LET *the* TENACITY *of* MATTIE FISHER INSPIRE YOU

BELIEVE
in the
MAGIC

I0152442

DEE LOUIS-SCOTT

Published by DocUmeant *Publishing*
244 5th Ave, Ste G-200
NY, NY 10001

646-233-4366

Unless otherwise noted, all Scriptures are taken from the Holy Bible, King
James Version.

Denise Michaels
InnerWorks Enterprises
Editor

http://mentoringwithdenise.com/

Ruth Ramsey
Ramsey & Associates Design, Inc.
Cover Design

Ginger Marks
DocUmeant Designs
Assistant Editor, Design & Layout

www.DocUmeantDesigns.com

Printed in the United States of America
ISBN 13: 978-1-937801-22-9 (print)

In Memory of
Mom & Dad

Dedication

For Autumn.

CONTENTS

TABLE OF FIGURES

FOREWORD

Blazing a new trail, Mattie Fisher left the South, moved north and managed to help some of her family move north, too. Thank God she had the chutzpah to leave the south and reach back for her sisters and brothers to follow her to the Midwest. All my family, including George, Uncle Alfred, cousins and their family's lives would have been so different were it not for our Aunt Mattie.

Life was not easy in the beginning for the family in Kansas City. When I was a toddler, my mom could not take care of her children financially. My siblings were sent to an orphanage. I was too young to go; so Aunt Mattie stepped up and took me in. Through her generosity, she helped me escape the trauma my older sibling experienced. Eventually we were reunited with my mom, but Aunt Mattie continued to be a strong force in my life.

I love to say, "My mother raised me, and Aunt Mattie 'groomed' me." Aunt Mattie had an enormous impact throughout my life. Through her example she showed me, I could be an independent woman without relying on a man. I can remember her driving a car by herself. As a child in the projects in the 50s, I never saw a black woman driving, let alone driving without someone else in the car.

Aunt Mattie let me know by telling me, encouraging me, and showing me through her own life I didn't have to follow the status quo. She told me I didn't have to settle for becoming a maid; I could become a professional career woman. After I graduated high school in 1964, I had no idea what to do. She told my mom I should go to secretarial school and even found the school in downtown Kansas City, Missouri.

When my Mom died in 1970 I was devastated. I told myself I could get through it because Aunt Mattie would still be there for me.

Throughout my life as I waded through unchartered waters, Aunt Mattie was there as a positive influence, encouraging me to take chances and believe in myself. I retired a few years ago as a Business Manager at the University of Missouri Kansas City campus. In 1964 I could have never pictured that career path. Aunt Mattie always knew.

She refused to be boxed in. And, she never accepted the limits others tried to place on her. Aunt Mattie made us BELIEVE that anything was possible. She truly helped us to *Believe in the Magic.*

Janet Williams

Acknowledgments

Mom and Dad thank you for giving me life.

Robert Williams Jr., Squirt loves you very much. Our time together, as brother and sister, was short but the memories will always loom large in my life.

Thank you, my baby girl, Autumn for your love and support. They were times when you became the mom in this emotional journey we both took with this book.

Janet Williams, Audrey (Sis) and Wilma, thank you for your love and support. This book is completed because of the invaluable information you gave me.

Ralph Parker II, we love and miss you so much. We now live each day with purpose never taking life for granted.

Denise Michaels, my book mentor, editor, coach, sometimes psychologist, and sometimes spiritual advisor. Thank you for your time and patience this book could not have been completed without you.

Ramsey and Associates, thank you for the beautiful book cover. You captured the essences of my mom.

Ginger Marks, thank you for your patience and encouragement. Your layout and design work brought my book to life.

To my family and friends, thank you for your support.

INTRODUCTION

In 1976, I was 19 years old. My mom and I separated, moving into different homes for the first time. She moved into a senior citizen high-rise. I moved into an apartment close to the college I attended. We lived about five miles away from each other and decided to share our 1970 Ford Torino. I needed the car for school and my part time job. Mom knew she would never be trapped in her apartment thanks to the senior van that would provide shuttles three times a week. She also knew she could get a ride with one of the tenants.

By the fall of 1977 our old Torino was on its last leg. We said a prayer every time we stopped; to please let it start again. If it started we prayed again that it would make it to the next stop. We figured it would cost us about the same amount to fix it as it would take to buy a brand new car. If we fixed it would still be a seven-year-old car with high mileage. So mom announced we were going to go look for a new car, this time at a dealership.

Immediately I thought she meant one of those cash and drive it off the lot type of dealerships. I asked her where we would get the money to buy a car. She replied, "We're going to finance it." Mom reminded me; I needed a reliable car especially since I worked late evenings. She needed to know I would be safe. She planned on going car shopping the following Saturday morning.

That Saturday morning was a beautiful day. The sun was shining and there wasn't a cloud in the sky. As luck would have it the Ford Torino started without any problems that day. I picked up mom and we drove together to the Chevrolet dealership in Kansas City, Kansas. The Torino drove like a new car.

We pulled into the dealership on State Avenue where we were promptly greeted by a nice young salesman. Mom told him we wanted to look at a new car. After looking around, mom and I fell in love with a yellow Chevette. She told the salesman we wanted that one. The salesman took us inside to the office to fill out the paper work.

He asked Mom if we had a trade-in. "Probably not," she replied

Then we got to the all-important question of income. "Mrs. Brown, where do you work?" the salesman asked.

"I work for the Kansas City Kansas Housing Authority," she replied. She continued to explain she worked weekends only, a total of 16 hours a week. "I guess I make about $120 a month," she said.

The salesman looked puzzled and asked if mom had any other income.

She said, "Yes I'm on Social Security. That's $250 a month." Before the salesman could ask another question mom piped up, "I want my daughter's name on the car as well."

The salesman looked relieved as he asked me my name.

"D'Nita Louis," I responded.

Then he asked me the all-important question. "Miss Louis where do you work and what is your monthly income?"

"I'm a student," I replied. "I work part time about 15 hours a week at J.C. Penney. I make about $100 a month."

The salesman politely said, "Ladies, I'm sorry. I don't think our finance department will let you have a loan for this car with that income."

Mom politely answered, "You haven't asked them yet." She continued praising the young man saying, "You're a good salesman. I know you can talk to them into it."

The salesman tried to pull himself out of the equation telling mom he had nothing to do with it. It was not his decision.

Mom told him, "The car we came in is falling apart." Then she grabbed me by the hand and pulled me close to her saying, "My baby works nights. I need her to be safe. Just promise me you'll do your best."

"Yes ma'am I'll try," the salesman said as if he was looking at his own mother and sister.

Mom and I left the building hoping the Ford Torino would start. It did.

We spent the next two weeks waiting. I remember going to her apartment building. I found Mom in the lobby talking to other tenants in the building. Anxiously, I asked Mom if she had heard from the dealership about our car.

She replied, "No, not yet."

One of the busy body tenants spoke up. "You all are trying to buy a new car? They're not going to let you have a new car. My daughter and son-in-law have full-time jobs and they were turned down for a car loan."

Mom simply replied, "They haven't told us 'no' yet."

I tugged on mom's arm to get her away from the other tenants as we walked toward the building elevator. As the doors closed, I told mom some of the people at work said the same thing to me. There's no way we can get a new car. The elevator stopped on the ninth floor. We got out and walked down the hall in silence to mom's apartment.

As we walked into her apartment mom asked if I wanted something to drink. I said, "No thanks." I sat down on the sofa and picked up the conversation from the elevator. "Mom we need a Plan B. I don't think this will work. It's been a week already."

Mom asked, "What happened to you believing in the magic?"

I told her, "When I wonder if the old Torino will start so I can get to school, or, when I'm afraid it might stop in the middle of the street and I'm stranded, it's hard to believe in magic then."

"Have faith," Mom said "Never stop believing."

The phone rang. Mom got up to answer it. "Yes, this is she," I overheard. "Yes I had a 1968 Impala station wagon. Smith and Sons Motors. Yes okay, thank you."

She hung and explained it was our salesman wanting to know if we had financed another car. "We're going to get the car just like I told you!" Mom said, excited, her eyes glowing.

"Yeah, but did he say that mom? It sounded like he's just asking more questions, I sighed. "I'm going home now. I need to study." I got up and headed for the apartment door.

Mom called out to me, "Baby have faith. I know I taught you that. You must believe!"

"I'll try Mom." I said walking out the door. As I walked to the old car I tried to remember what mom had said. Once again, my focus shifted to the Torino. Please let this car start, I prayed silently.

About three weeks after our initial visit to the car dealership, mom called me on the phone. She spoke in a subdued voice.

"What time do you get out of school?" she asked. "Do you have to go to work?"

"No mom, why? Do you need to go somewhere?" I asked her.

"Yes. If you can we need to go to the dealership," she said, her voice still almost a whisper.

"What on earth do they need from us now," I asked in a sarcastic tone.

"They want us to pick up our new car!" she said, her volume increasing.

"What?"

Mom burst into laughter. "They want us to pick up our car!!"

I let out a scream so loud I know the residents over in the next apartment building had to hear me.

We picked our new, yellow 1977 Chevrolet Chevette the next day. We left the old, broken down Torino with the dealership and drove off the lot with our shiny new car.

We got so many questions from people asking, "How you all qualify for that new car?"

I would say, "Mom believed in the magic and I tried."

My mom, Mattie Pearl Fisher, always told me to believe in the magic. The magic meant miracles in action. The miracles of life can be big, small, and everything in between. Miracles are like magic. Those 'Wow Moments' when you just cannot believe what happened are revealed. She would tell me, "No matter how old you get, always look for, expect, and you will see the magic." Mom always kept the Holy Bible and *The Power of Positive Thinking* by Norman Vincent Peal on her nightstand next to her bed.

Most kids think their mom is the best. Of course I am no different. My mom was my best friend from a very young age onward. The older I get, the smarter I realize my mom truly was. Not one day goes by that I am not reminded of something, or think of something, she taught me. We went through so much together.

Originally my intention was to leave a historical record of Mattie Pearl Fisher's life for my daughter, Autumn. As I examined old notes and taped recordings, I knew the world had to hear her story. Mom's story is both powerful and inspirational.

In this book, you will follow mom through events of her life including the moment of her death.

Mattie Pearl was born at a time in history when being both a Negro and a woman was a double curse. You had to look very hard to find any human or legal rights. Despite all the obstacles, Mom always stood her ground. She was confident and fierce, always pushing forward, striving to do things important to her. More than once mom slammed the door right in the face of those who thought they could dictate her life. She had a tenacious spirit that was infectious to other women everywhere she went. Mom taught all women who encountered her to never settle for less than they deserved.

Like everyone else, mom's life was not perfect. Still the magic shown through in ways you would not imagine. Through marriages, divorces, betrayals and loss, Mom always found a way to rise and STAND. She stood not bitter, angry or vengeful but loving and forgiving.

At the end of each chapter you will discover life lessons. Lessons I hope will inspire you and others that will perhaps help you to avoid making the same mistakes as mom made.

I know my mom would want her life to inspire others. If she were here today she would say, "You can achieve whatever is in your heart."

Believe in that magic and be tenacious about getting it for yourself.

AHEAD OF HER TIME

"Whatever you do or dream you can do . . . begin it. Boldness has genius and power and magic in it." — J.W. von Goethe

Mattie Pearl Fisher was a black woman way ahead of her time. The early 20th century, was still a time when white males made all-important decisions. At a time when women, especially black women, did not have many rights, she stood strong in the face of all adversity.

Mattie was forward-thinking, confident; fiercely independent, high spirited, and advanced in her ideas and actions. She taught all women who came in contact with her to be strong, to never settle for less than they deserved in life.

When Mattie lost her grandparents, she was forced to move back to her mother's house. Her mother had remarried,and had two younger children with her new husband. Mattie's grandparents had spoiled her, so she was not used to sharing anything with anybody. Her grandparents owned their land free and clear in "name of state." Her grandfather and farmer's helper produced and sold cotton, dairy and cattle products. After her grandparent's death the land was not passed on to her mother. Whites in the area pushed backed against black land owners with threats of violence.

Suddenly she had two half-siblings and a stepfather. Her relationship with her stepfather was a combative one.

Mattie's mother and stepfather were cotton sharecroppers. They raised cotton on the plantation of white landowners back in the 1920s.

The sharecropping system was a financially oppressive one. Often it enslaved the sharecroppers financially even if they were not enslaved legally. Under this arrangement, landowners supplied the sharecropper with land, housing, tools, and seeds. The landowner assumed chief supervision of the farming operations and also retained legal rights to all the crops. Sharecroppers brought only their labor to the bargaining table to create income.

After the harvest at the end of the growing season, the sharecropper was paid a share of the produce grown in lieu of cash wages. They typically received about one-third to one-half of the crops as payment. Sharecroppers were responsible for their own food and clothing. Often the amount owed to the land owner at 'settling time' at the end of the season exceeded the value of their share of the crop. The family often asked the landowner for credit which resulted in keeping them bound financially. Thus, Mattie's family seemed to be in a perpetual cycle of debt.

Even as a child Mattie knew this system was not right. She would rebel against picking the cotton. One day when she was only 12 years old, her anger at her stepfather and the unfair system finally came to a head.

As Mattie was picking cotton in the sweltering heat, she noticed Mr.Douce, the landowner, sitting on his horse beside her.

"You ain't doin' that right, gurl," he said criticizing her.

"I hate you," she replied under her breath.

"What you say, gurl?" Mr. Douce asked her.

Mattie stayed silent.

"I'm talking to you, gurl. I asked you a question," Mr. Douce prodded her.

Suddenly, Mattie lost her temper. Grabbing the hoe and screaming wildly, she swung the hoe around chopping all the cotton into small pieces. Her parents came anxiously running through the fields, unaware of what was going on.

"Mattie Pearl, what's goin' on?" her mother asked.

Mr. Douce dismounted his horse. "You better talk to that gurl of yours," he said.

"I hate him! I hate him!" Mattie screamed, seething with anger.

Looking around at the mess she made of the cotton, her mother screamed back, "Are you crazy? What have you done?"

Her mother wrapped her arms around her while moving quickly, almost dragging Mattie back to the house. Her stepfather tried to cool things down with Mr.Douce.

Still weeping uncontrollably she tried to explain. "He was standing over me with that gun like I was some kind of animal. I can't stand it anymore momma," she cried.

Her mother tried to explain she was only hurting everyone by chopping up the cotton. "When you chopped up that cotton you just hurt the family. Now we have to pay for it."

Mattie sobbed loudly, "I'm never gonna pick cotton. Never gonna pick cotton ever again. I hate it!"

Her stepfather came in screaming at her, "Gurl you cost us a lot of money!" he bellowed. "Now you gonna have to work twice as hard to pay it off."

Sniffling she repeated, "I'm never gonna pick cotton again," this time for her stepfather.

"Well, you not gonna stay here without working," her stepfather replied.

Tempers slowly calmed. Mattie, her mother, and her oldest half-sister started preparing dinner. She spoke very few words that evening as her stepfather's words kept running through her mind.

She knew she had to make a decision.

The next morning her parents prepared for another day toiling in the cotton fields. Mattie's half-siblings were off to school. She stayed in bed, explaining to her mother she was really ill. Her mother sensed she was lying, but she covered for her anyway with her stepfather.

Her stepfather screamed, "She lyin'! You know that gurl's lyin'!"

Mattie lay there listening to the argument from her bed. She felt guilty about putting her mother in such a difficult situation with her husband. It seemed like forever, but eventually they left for the fields for the day.

Once again she started sobbing uncontrollably. She felt like her existence made things hard on the family especially her mother. Her stepfather made her feel like an outsider. He treated her differently from his own children. She knew exactly what she had to do. She had to LEAVE!

After a quick meal, she packed her clothes and a few essential items in a feed sack. Walking outside the house, she got as far as the first steps to the porch. Raising her head in

4

resolve, she looked up to her awaiting future. Instantaneously, Mattie saw her mother walking back toward the house. Promptly, she dropped the feed sack on the side of the steps and turned sideways to block her mother from noticing the sack of traveling items.

"Mattie Pearl, are you feeling better?" her mother asked.

"Momma, I got something to tell you." She breathed deeply and said, "I'm leaving."

"What you mean you leavin'?" her mother asked.

"I can't live like this, mother." Mattie explained she did not want to hurt the family. Starting to cry again, she laid it on the line. She said her stepfather didn't want her in the house and he treated her differently from her half-siblings. She also repeated her conversation from the day before, once again refusing to pick cotton ever again. She also talked about the oppressive Mr.Douce riding over her and looking down at her like she was an animal.

Mattie reached down and grabbed the feed sack she dropped a few minutes before from the side of the steps. "I love you, mother. But I got to go."

Her mother began to cry, but soon her tears turned to anger. "If you leave you not gonna 'mount to nothin', gurl. You hear me, Mattie Pearl!"

She turned around, briefly acknowledging her mother's words. "I guess I won't 'mount to nothin' then." Mattie Pearl proceeded down the dusty road away from the farm for the last time.

In the midst of the Great Depression when unemployment neared 25 percent, at age 17, Mattie lived a good life. She found domestic work in Baton Rouge for a wealthy husband and wife in their 50s. The family treated her with respect. She had her own room in their mansion, beautifully decorated with her own bathroom.

Since the family had no children, the Missus took Mattie under her wing teaching her all types of proper etiquette from setting a formal dinner table to table manners and proper diction. The Missus loved to sew. She made Mattie's clothing and nice things for her room. Mattie even learned how to drive the family car. She would drive it alone to the city to pick up whatever the family needed.

The Mister on the other hand, had a wandering eye and hands. Over time, Mattie became increasingly uncomfortable around him. He would give her hugs and pats on the back. Then it became more intimate, touching her butt and breasts.

She would pull away from him saying, "No, sir."

He always reminded her how much he had done for her. The Mister thought so, at least.

One evening after the Missus retired to the study for some reading, he approached Mattie while she was cleaning.

"I see you'll be busy for a while yet tonight. Be ready tomorrow, I'm coming to your room." he told her with a sly smirk.

"No sir. I don't want you to." she pleaded.

"You'll be glad I did. Just wait and see." he insisted.

Afraid of being raped, Mattie made her exit plan overnight. Without a word she left the next morning before they woke up. After more than six years, Mattie left what was otherwise a very comfortable situation. In that time, she had grown from a poor country girl into a sophisticated, refined young lady.

If you were to ask her how she survived The Great Depression, she always said, "What depression? I never knew there was one."

In the 1940s armed with a newer, stronger sense of self, Mattie started developing her entrepreneurial spirit.

She moved from Baton Rouge to Arkansas. Moving around from Little Rock, Hot Springs, Malvern, Arkadelphia, she eventually settled down in Texarkana. In each city she found jobs cooking food, sometimes in well-to-do homes, other times in bar-and-grill type restaurants or serving drinks in juke joints.

One day while having Sunday dinner at a café, mom had an idea. She loved cooking and she thought she could do something on her own.

She found a large house to rent. She wanted to live upstairs and use the downstairs as a snack shop. So, with permission from the owner, Mattie—a young black woman—went into business for herself. She owned a snack shop offering sandwiches, soda and candy for kids after school.

Mattie loved music and she knew the young people would love it, too. So, a few weeks later she added a jukebox to attract the youngsters to come and stay a little longer.

On Sundays, she prepared dinner for the after church crowd. Her café was called Mattie's. She serves up Southern Cuisine including fried chicken, pork chops, yams, greens and cornbread.

Mattie's was a successful venture and profitable from the start. Friends told her she should stay open longer hours after the school kids left on Fridays and Saturday nights to make even more money serving dinners. Mom wanted to serve alcohol to the adults, but she knew she would never get approval for a liquor license as a black person and a woman.

So, what's a girl to do? She sold booze anyway under the table to customers.

All went well for the first few months. Finally, word leaked to the authorities, and the police started sniffing around. Mattie received threats not only from the police but also from the Ku Klux Klan. Some of the local residents discovered mom was making really good money in her business. They were talking to the authorities, too.

Finally, she confessed to the pastor of the church she occasionally attended. The pastor helped her get out of the house and let her stay with his family for a spell. Mattie knew she had to get out of town, so she contacted a family friend who had moved further north.

Look out Kansas City, here she comes.

Mattie's job in Kansas City was working at Macy's downtown store in the Dining Room as a Salad Girl. After a while she moved to the position of Assistant in Fabrics. She was very proud of her job in the Fabric Department. Though she only had a fourth-grade education, she beat out other applicants who had college degrees for the job. She was an incredibly capable, well-organized woman.

Mattie's personality suited her astrological sign, Taurus the Bull. She was outspoken, headstrong and wouldn't hesitate giving you a piece of her mind if she thought you were mistaken—according to Mattie. Her personality led her to another opportunity, spying. The Macy's Store Manager periodically asked her to shop at the competitors stores in Kansas City to see what their prices were for the same merchandise.

After my birth, and a divorce, she returned to that entrepreneurial spirit. She needed a way to earn money and be at home with me. She first went to Cosmetology School and eventually opened a beauty shop in her house. When her business slowed down she ran a daycare and took care of children to supplement her income.

Mattie's daycare reflected her love for children. She was a caring, loving person. She was also a disciplinarian with a gentle touch. The daycare grew so fast through word of mouth around the neighborhood, coupled with personal issues; she gradually had to give up the hair salon.

Eventually we outgrew our house. So, Mattie decided to move to a bigger, more versatile home. She rented out our Vineyard Woods home.

We moved to the inner city of Kansas City, to a home large enough to actually run a licensed daycare center. Our home was on the second level. She even rented out the one-bedroom apartment with a side entrance.

Mattie hired two helpers and split them up depending on the age of the children. Her weekday routine was to pick-up some of the daycare children in our station wagon. She had two shifts. Then she took the school age kids to their individual schools.

Around 11:00 am she picked up the kindergarteners. Then around 3:00 pm she would start her pick-up duties from the neighborhood schools. By 5:30 pm, she started taking the children home. Her day ended at about 7:00 pm. Yes, all this in rain, sleet, freezing rain and snow. She also served as her own accountant.

Her daycare center was very successful; unfortunately, all that prosperity came at the expense of her health. She was now in her mid-50s and the stress was affecting her health. The doctor said her blood pressure was too high. He told her she had a choice; either continue on this path and risk a stroke or scale back her life. She chose life, of course.

Mattie whittled down her daycare center to only six children and the State of Missouri paid for them.

Eventually the state checks and double checks, the rules and regulations and "the white glove test" as she called it were all too much for her. Finally, she closed her daycare center for good and we moved back to our Vineyard Woods home again.

Once we moved back to Vineyard Woods, Mattie put feelers out again for customers for her home hair salon. She said she only wanted five or six regular customers. She did a good job managing her money and saving. The daycare made on average about $300.00 per week after expenses, plus the side apartment rental. We lived well for the next few years.

★   ★   ★

Life Lessons

Mattie was so driven and daring, she never cared that the world was not quite ready for her indomitable spirit. The knowledge she gained, she generously shared with the women in our family. An important role for her was that of counselor. Her counsel was sometimes diplomatic. Other times she was direct with 100 percent honesty. Even though the opportunities back then were limited for black women, she would tell us how to navigate stealthily around the limited opportunities.

There are so many more career and business opportunities today compared to when my mother lived. I can hardly imagine what she could have accomplished if she were alive today.

Typically, race, gender, education and class shape and limit the life experiences for most people. This fact has been widely documented. Mom, however, was not typical in any way. She refused to let those boundaries shape her and her world. She tried to live her life without the limits society imposed on her back in the day.

"It's impossible," said pride.

"It's risky," said experience.

"It's pointless," said reason.

"Give it a try," whispered the heart."

These statements are often said in terms of finding love, but I believe it's true about life as well.

Dream the impossible dream. Take risks. It's never pointless. Try it. Never give up. If you give up you will never know what is possible.

It's Possible: Mom always said, "All things are possible as long as you believe it." To achieve a dream, you must first be willing to dream it. Look inside yourself, be honest with yourself, and know your dreams are powerful if you give them a chance. Today we understand in-depth the mind-body connection. We know what you imagine in your mind can become reality if you believe.

No one can dream your dreams for you; therefore, no one can tell you it will not come to fruition. The Creator has placed a dream, vision, and goals in your heart. Never give up on them. Dare to go ahead and dream the impossible dream. Demand the impossible.

Take Risks: There come times in everyone's life when you are faced with an important choice that involves risk. Mattie was risk taker. From the time she left home at the tender age of 12, throughout her entire life she took big risks. She just put herself out there. Whatever she did, she jumped in with both feet. Risk is by nature, a scary thing. It's uncertain and unpredictable. Don't be afraid to fail. Don't be afraid to take risks. Progress always involves risks.

Many great ideas have been lost forever because the people who had them could not risk criticism and humiliation if they failed. Anyone who has pursued their dreams and failed has lived much more than those who have put their dreams on a shelf for fear of failure. Taking a chance gives you the opportunity to open up to your dreams. It teaches you to set goals and follow through with your ideas. Risk allows you to make things happen rather than waiting for them to happen. You finally grow and discover new things about yourself and the world. Risk is exhilarating. It makes you feel alive. Be brave and chart your own path however risky.

It's Never Pointless: Everyone from Benjamin Franklin to Steve Jobs has been told their dreams or ideas were pointless. They were merely ahead of their times. Throughout history, so-called "experts" in their fields have told big dreamers that what they were dreaming was impossible. Do whatever it takes to make your dreams come true.

What is the worst that can happen, failure? Then learn from your mistakes. Keep going and growing. Develop greater strength and resolve. Whether you succeed or fail, the attempt to live your dreams will stretch you and give you faith in your strength and abilities. You will have confidence to do even more.

Try it: We all had ideas and dreams when we were kids. When people asked you, "What do you want to do when you grow up?" We wanted to do something that excited us and that we were passionate about. So, what happened? Why did we grow up and lose all the passion, the energy, and the strength to keep our dreams alive?

It is our fear of failure that makes us play it safe. That fear allows us to make excuses for why we cannot have all that we want. Excuses like:

☐ I don't have the time

☐ I have a family

☐ I need more money . . .

Those excuses help convince us that it is okay to hide from our dreams. Guess what? The only thing holding you back are the excuses you keep telling yourself about why you can't have what you want.

Life does not come with a guarantee in writing. This, of course, makes it risky and scary. But it is also what makes it interesting, exciting, and fun. Mentally go through your life. The parts that stand out are never the safe ones. The shining memories will always be the times when you took a leap of faith, whether you won the game or not.

Set big goals for yourself. Review them often. Believe your goals as the truth. Then watch what happens. Do whatever it takes to make your dreams come true. When you really believe, the universe always conspires to make that dream come true. Learn to use your voice now.

Believe!

"It's impossible," said pride.

"It's risky," said experience.

"It's pointless," said reason.

"Give it a try," whispered the heart."

★   ★   ★

RUN GET OUT NOW

*"Run don't walk. Your present circumstances don't determine
where you can go; they merely determine where you start."*
—Nido Qubein

Screaming in pain she passed out and stopped breathing. As
she told family many times, her recently deceased sister's spirit
came to her during childbirth and told her not to stop breathing.
Finally, she started breathing again.

It was 28 years since she felt that pain.

Mattie and John were married five uneventful years when I
came into the world Mattie and John were ages 43 and 57,
respectively. I was born at Phyllis Wheatley Hospital, one of the
"Negro" hospitals in Kansas City. I was definitely a surprise
baby. Mattie told her mother she thought she was going through
menopause.

My Grandmother told her, "No you're pregnant."

Mattie replied, "If I am, I'm going to jump off a bridge."

Grandmother's response, "Well, you better start jumpin'."

Both my parents had good jobs, excellent really considering
their race in the 1950s. Mattie's husband, John, worked his way

up through the company to become a Meat Inspector for the Amour Meat Packing Company.

Mattie was a Salad Girl in the dining room at Macy's and moved to the position of Assistant in Fabrics. She was very proud of her job in the Fabric department. Though she held only a fourth-grade education, she beat out other applicants for the position with college degrees. Mattie Pearl was an incredibly capable, well-organized woman. She was outspoken, headstrong and wouldn't hesitate giving you a piece of her mind if she thought you were mistaken—in her opinion.

I was brought from the hospital into my new home in a middle-class neighborhood in the heart of the city. The house was a deep rose color with a large front porch that extended the full length of the house. My favorite room in that house was my bedroom, which was filled with stuffed animals, dolls, and games. The back porch was screened-in and overlooked a lush vegetable garden which made my father very proud. The detached one car garage housed his hunting equipment, lawn mower and gardening supplies. The family cars were always parked in the driveway by the back porch.

Mattie had one other child, a son named Robert, with whom she had a close bond. He was 28, married, and had a two-year old daughter when I was born. Robert and I were half-siblings and had different fathers. It didn't seem to matter. John loved my brother, his wife Audrey, and their little daughter all living together under one roof in the rose-colored house. It was wonderful having everyone together to pitch in until my parents were settled into a routine with me, their brand-new baby daughter.

It was Robert and his wife Audrey's idea to move out a few months after I was born. That way my parents would have more privacy raising their new daughter and being a family unit together.

After a few months on maternity leave, Mattie went back to her job at Macy's. She always cared about making her own money. That's what happens when you leave your parents' home at the tender age of twelve. Gradually Mattie's husband pressured her to give up her career and be a full-time stay-at-home-mom. She didn't want to do it at first, she was fiercely self-reliant. But she complied with her husband's wishes and quickly devoted all her time to being at home with me.

Perhaps it was the pressure of supporting and raising a small child and Mattie's focus on her new baby that left John feeling out on the fringes of the family. Life was about to get dangerous.

⁓⁓✿⁓⁓⁓✿⁓⁓⁓✿⁓⁓

The happiest times I remember with my parents took place every Sunday evening. We would all watch, "Walt Disney's Wonderful World of Color" followed by "Bonanza." I loved the opening theme song to Bonanza; and had a little pony dance my parents loved to watch. I remember their big smiles and laughter. We all ate ice cream sodas while we enjoyed the show. Sadly, this is the only happy memory I have of my parents together.

It started out like any other weekday morning, the hustle and bustle of everyone rushing to get out of the house on time. Mattie was back in school. She wanted a job that allowed her to work from home. So, she enrolled in Cosmetology School. Hurrying down the stairs toward the front door, she reached into the familiar silver bowl for her car keys, but they were missing.

She looked puzzled and slightly dazed. Remember, she was always very well-organized.

When she arrived each evening, she dropped her keys in a special spot, the silver bowl by the front door. Misplacing an important item like keys was not like her at all. She rushed around panicked. She raced up and down the stairs twice, but the keys were not to be found.

John was the hero that morning, finding Mattie's keys in the refrigerator. A few days went by without incident, and then it happened again. No keys. There was a look of hurt on my mother's face. At age three, I tried to console her.

John found the keys again, this time in her dresser drawer. It began happening once, maybe twice a week. At this point, she would put my barrettes in the silver bowl with the keys for extra marking. Still, the keys would disappear along with the barrettes by the next morning.

Every time John would be the hero and find Mattie's keys in some obscure place. My hair barrettes were always discovered placidly laying on my dresser.

Eventually, Mattie became frantic about her keys. It was not the person I had known up until then. She started sleeping with them clutched in her hand. Our morning routine gradually included gripping the car keys tightly while getting ready for the day.

As small child, I stayed at my brother Robert's home during the day. Mattie's Cosmetology school was located not far from home.

Late one afternoon exhausted from standing on her feet all day, she left school to discover her car was not where she parked it that morning.

She screamed, "My car is gone! Someone stole my car." In a fright she rushed back inside to call John who promptly called the police.

John and the police officer arrived about the same time. As the police officer approached Mattie his brow was furrowed with mock concern.

What's going on?

Mattie showed them where she parked her car and gave them all the relevant information. John drove Mattie home, belittling her all the way. A couple hours later, the police arrived at our house with news. They found the car parked two blocks away from the school untouched.

With a smug grin the officer said, "You must have forgotten where you parked it."

She tried to logically explain she wouldn't park her car two blocks away when the parking lot was right behind the school building. Mattie was being her outspoken self, but her confidence was waning. They wrote her off as a hysterical, crazy lady.

Gradually, more things disappeared when she laid them down. John would insult her every time. He would even get in her face yelling at her. But he always backed down if he saw me come into the room.

Misplacing items were happening more. There were many nights when she literally cried herself to sleep, asking God not to let her lose her mind because she had child to raise.

Mattie leaned heavily on her best friend Anita, explaining she was afraid she was losing her mind. The confident, independent, outspoken woman who gave birth to me had transformed into a frightened woman, afraid she was losing her mental abilities. The most painful part was that the man she counted on the most, her husband, was becoming so cruel. After a while Mattie surmised; maybe she deserved it. Anita was always comforting to Mattie, like an angel sent from God.

The physical abuse started with pushing. Screaming in her face, "You crazy bitch!" he shoved her against the wall. He belittled her constantly reminding her how uneducated she was. He always put her down; repeating that many of the women in his family had college degrees. He never let her forget no one in her family ever finished college.

His ear-piercing outbursts struck her as rational and understandable at this stage. He was always coming to her rescue because she was stupid, she thought. "How long can he put up with me?" she wondered.

Eventually pushing turned into punches. There were late night car trips to my Aunt Willie Mae's house, only to return home the next day. She promised herself she would try better to not do anything that might upset him. Not only was Mattie convinced she was losing her mind, she also was convinced she didn't deserve any better than a husband who had become a batterer. It was as if she was living her life walking on eggshells during those early years of my life.

One night after a punch that resulted in Mattie landing at the bottom of a flight of stairs, something snapped inside her. She looked up at her husband standing over her. Despite her pain, she came up swinging with a right hook, hitting her husband in the nose.

He was stunned.

A tussle broke out with both parents bleeding and rolling on the floor. Once again, she scooped me up late that night fleeing to Willie Mae's house again only to return home the next day.

The scariest moment for me involved a knife. I can still see myself trying to pull my father by his underwear off my mom.

She told me, "Call the operator like I taught you."

I dialed "0" on the telephone and told the operator, through my tears and screaming, my parents were fighting with a knife. I ran back into the room and kept screaming, hitting John in the back. He was so startled; they just stopped fighting. No one got hurt physically, but the emotional bruises lasted a lifetime.

When the police officer finally arrived he said, "Okay, so if you two were fighting, who called the police?"

I spoke up and replied, "Me!"

He asked, "How old are you?"

"Four," I replied.

The police officer chastised both my parents for their behavior. "You should be ashamed of yourselves, fighting in front of a child like that."

One day Mattie was washing clothes. She pulled the clothes out of John's hunting bag. Years later she told me the lady's underwear in the bag had blood stains on it from menstruation. Suspicious, she began to watch his every move.

Late one night, he made an excuse to leave the house. Looking just like an experienced super sleuth, she followed him with me in tow. She was stunned when he arrived at her best friend Anita's house. Looking very confused, she tried to give them the benefit of the doubt. Maybe Anita was trying to talk to him to see what was going on.

We sat parked up the street from the house for a few minutes, and then took a quiet drive back home. We could hear the midnight chimes of the grandfather clock as we arrived home. It was too late for my bath; I knew the drill from our night flights to Willie Mae's. I said my prayers and was off to bed. I heard her soft cries as I tried to drift off to sleep in my bedroom. Why wasn't he home yet? Next day, she waited on a confession from either of them. A confession she did not receive.

One night Mattie grabbed me from my bed out of a deep sleep and rushed me into the car. We were following him again. The motion of the car sent me back to sleep. I awoke when the car stopped, only one house away from Anita's. This time we sat for what seemed like hours. I peppered her with questions, most of them went unanswered.

Finally, the door to her house opened. Anita emerged in her nightgown in the dark night air with John. At that moment, she ordered me to lie down on the seat. I think she wanted to protect me from seeing what I later learned was a passionate kiss between John and Mattie's best friend, Anita. Apparently, he was so engrossed in that kiss he didn't notice whose car was pulling away. It seemed like we arrived home just a few minutes before he did.

He walked through the door to our rose-colored house and she confronted him. Screaming at the top of her lungs she announced her intention to divorce him. She told John she knew all his dirty little secrets. Near hysterics, she revealed she knew of his affair with Anita.

"How could you do this to me?" she wailed.

Eerily calm, John fired back at her, "No I'm divorcing you". He threw out the name of a lawyer he already retained.

I expected to see a blood bath, but it didn't happen this time. She slept in the bed in my room with me after that argument.

Mattie only thought she knew all John's dirty little secrets.

One night according to Mattie, the bed shook violently. Focusing intently, she heard John talking on the phone. At first she thought it was Anita on the other end of the line, but the conversation had a different tone. She crept to the door and slowly opened it.

She heard John brag, telling the caller how glad he was to have him as his attorney. What could possibly be so important that early in the morning? She continued listening intently to the conversation between John and his attorney. Later, she always said it was magic that she awoke in the middle of the night just at the right time to hear the conversation. She had always been a heavy sleeper.

John and his attorney were discussing getting commitment papers for her. As she listened further, she was horrified to learn he was behind everything that made her doubt herself and her sanity over the last few years. He explained to the attorney in great detail about hiding things, including her car keys to confuse her and make her doubt herself.

He thought it was brilliant that he arranged to have her car moved and a Police Report filed for evidence. He even had a witness, her best friend. Her best friend Anita, whom she had confessed to, would verify everything.

All these elaborate steps were an attempt to drive Mattie crazy and get custody of me in a divorce.

★　　★　　★

Life Lessons

Mattie would say, "Never make the same mistakes I did."

Be financially independent: She told me to never become reliant upon anyone, not even your husband. Mattie said first, don't become too dependent, especially financially dependent on anyone. Make sure you always generate an income on your own.

There are so many more options for women today. Even if you are a stay-at-home mom while your kids are small, find a way to generate an income of your own. For instance, start a daycare, a paid car pool, take a hobby and turn it into a business. Be creative. Always keep a personal checking and saving account that is just yours. Take a percentage of your earned income and put it in your personal account. Take the remainder of your income and use it to contribute to the household expenses you and your partner agree on.

So, in my marriage I was upfront with my husband, telling him I needed to maintain my own accounts. I told him I thought he should do the same. I explained that I did not like having to ask permission to buy something or do something. I also knew we both brought separate debt to the marriage, so we should pay that debt from our personal checking accounts. I asked that we come up with an equitable percentage we could put into our joint bank account. That way the transition was smooth.

Never let anyone else make all the decisions for you and your life. You should always be a part of the decision-making process. When you earn your own money, and even if you don't, you still contribute toward the household. You are definitely entitled to help make decisions. After all it is a partnership.

Think about your children: Mattie knew it was hard for me. I witnessed things between my parents a child should not see. She would say, "Never put your child through this." I know she tried to do the right thing. The scars have lasted throughout my lifetime. As a child, I wonder why my parents stayed together when they were so unhappy. A common feeling I think many parents have is that it is better to stay together for the sake of the children. I can tell you this is so wrong.

Like most children, I preferred my parent just separate and put an end to all the emotional and physical abuse. Many children who witness the abuse of their mothers demonstrate significant behavioral and/or emotional problems as children and later in life as adults. Fortunately, I was not one of those children. Instead, once I became an adult, I was determined not to live the same way my parents did.

Fight Fair: When you see the relationship turning nasty, including verbal and emotional abuse, just stop. Try to talk to each other about fighting fair. If that doesn't work find someone professional to talk with about your issues. If the fighting ever escalates and becomes physical, leave; period!

No one should ever control what you do; who you see or talk to; or where you go. You should never be forced to give up anything that is a positive influence in your life. Why would anyone who loves you want you to give up something positive?

What is Abuse? Abuse is the act, practice, use or treatment of a person that causes damage to that person. Abuse can come in the form of verbal abuse, emotional abuse, psychological abuse, financial abuse, sexual abuse and/or physical abuse. Abuse does not discriminate against gender, race, socio economic status, marital status, or age.

In the beginning, John used indirect forms of Psychological/Emotional Abuse disguised as "helping" the person who was being abused, Mattie.

Psychological and Emotional abuse is rarely talked about. A major aspect of this type of abuse is secrecy. John knew Mattie would never want my brother Robert or any other family members to know about what was happening behind the doors of our house. Also, her pride would not let her tell anyone. Finally, she confided in her best friend, Anita. Mattie was always considered the tough one in the family. She felt like she could handle any situation. She was embarrassed that she couldn't handle it.

Mattie's mental anguish as a result of the abuse she suffered at her husband's hands lingered with her for the rest of her life. Anytime anything, especially her keys, went missing, she would sweat and shake profusely. The aim of psychological/ emotional abuse is to chip away at a person's feelings of self-worth and independence.

Mattie's physical abuse happened after her spirit was crushed by the on-going psychological and emotional abuse. Her husband, as the abuser, set her up so he could put his plan in motion, creating a situation where he could eventually justify physically abusing her.

Are you in an abusive relationship? Does your partner:

☐ Embarrass you with put-downs?

☐ Look at you or act in ways that scare you?

☐ Control what you do, who you see or talk to or where you go?

☐ Prevent you from seeing your friends or family members?

☐ Take your money, make you ask for money or refuse to give you money?

☐ Make all of the decisions in the relationship?

☐ Tell you you're a bad parent, or, threaten to take away or hurt your children?

☐ Prevent you from working or attending school?

☐ Act like the abuse is no big deal, it's your fault, or even denies doing it?

☐ Destroy your property or threaten to kill your pets?

☐ Intimidate you with guns, knives or other weapons?

☐ Shove you, slap you, choke you, or hit you?

☐ Force you to try and drop charges?

☐ Threaten to commit suicide?

☐ Threaten to kill you?

If you answered 'yes' to even one of these questions, you may be in an abusive relationship. Support from others who care can make a big difference in your life. Tell at least two or three people the truth of what is happening in your relationship.

Mattie told only her sister Willie Mae about the physical abuse. Aunt Willie Mae was a very passive person and she knew her sister would keep quiet. Anita, the woman she thought was her best friend only knew about the verbal abuse.

Leave the relationship! If you are not strong enough to get out immediately, construct a safety plan and gradually work on getting out.

Your safety plan should start with recognizing and trying to prevent other incidents of violence. Based on the abuser's previous behaviors, try to find a way to calm the situation when things get heated. Some examples might be: Try going to another room, getting busy doing something else, ignore the abuser, or remain quiet. Have a plan of action if that does not work and the situation escalates further. Attempt to leave the house, go to a pre-designated place and call 911.

Things to be aware of and keep in a safe place:

☐ Location of all phones and exits in the house.

☐ Domestic Violence Hotline 800-537-2238 or your local hotline number.

☐ Safety and care of children.

☐ An extra set of keys to the car.

☐ Hidden emergency money.

☐ Copies of important documents and papers like birth certificates, passports

☐ List of possible alternative living arrangements.

☐ A hidden pre-packed suitcase.

☐ Check books, bank books, credit cards, or at least their account numbers.

☐ All social security number for yourself, including the abusers and the children.

☐ All needed medications.

Seek out legal support and other professionals. You need to build a support system of legal professionals and a therapist. If you cannot afford an attorney, Legal Aid in your city can help you. The police department can help you file a Domestic Violence Complaint and obtain a Temporary Restraining Order. The Restraining Order will provide protection under the law.

You can also ask for:

☐ That the abuser be removed from the home and kept from returning

☐ Possession of the residence without harassment by the abuser

☐ Custody of your children

☐ Some type of temporary financial support

☐ Professional counseling for you, the children and the abuser

☐ Monetary compensation for your expenses.

Life versus material possessions: While the Temporary Restraining Order works the majority of the time, in some situations an abuser is so violent; the protection order becomes just a piece of paper. In this situation, do not rely upon it as your sole means of protection. If you are in danger, find a safe place to stay. This means leaving the bulk of your material possessions and your familiar environment. Although it may seem unfair because you are the victim and you are vested in the relationship and your home, chose your life and the life of your children over your material possessions.

Things to do after you leave.

☐ Keep your new location a secret.

☐ Get an unlisted phone number.

☐ Use a post office box rather than your home address.

☐ Apply to your state's Address Confidentiality Program, a service that confidentially forwards your mail to your home.

☐ Cancel your shared old bank accounts and credit cards

☐ Open new accounts; be sure to use a different bank.

Realize you deserve a healthy relationship. One that is free from abuse. A healthy relationship is based on the belief that both partners are equals. Each of you should retain the ability to listen in an open-minded manner, respecting your differences and supporting the feelings of the other. A healthy relationship holds a commitment to support each other in life. It also includes encouraging each other to be independent. It means communicating openly and truthfully, admitting when you are wrong or have made mistakes. Most importantly, making sure each person feels safe in the relationship both through words and actions.

Empower yourself with new skills, knowledge and creativity. Dare to dream! Now is the time to look at your dreams again. Think about the skills you need to make your dreams come true. What are your hobbies and interests? Make sure you allow yourself to indulge in "you" things.

Take back control of your life! Never forget, there is magic in the smallest things. A moment of clarity, whether in your own thoughts or over-hearing someone else's conversation, is a gift to be appreciated.

★　　　★　　　★

DIRTY DEEDS . . . AND STILL I STAND

"Divorce isn't such a tragedy. A tragedy's staying in an unhappy marriage, teaching your children the wrong things about love. Nobody ever died of divorce." — Jennifer Weiner

"No, sorry I can't help," the attorney's voice boomed. Adding, "You should know you're gonna have a hard time finding someone to work with you."

When Mattie asked why, he stared away. Confused, she turned on her heel and walked out of the office.

The attorney with the booming voice was right. Mattie heard the word "no" from other attorneys over and over. Other times, she left phone messages with receptionists for attorneys; she never got a return call. Months later her call would finally be returned informing her that the attorney could not take the case. The attorney's reason? All he could say in reply was, "It's complicated."

Her divorce case was a subject of gossip for a tightly knit group of attorneys in Kansas City that served the Negro community. Somehow they all knew this was going to be a nasty case. Not a single attorney in the clique wanted to be on the losing end of a long, protracted fight.

Apparently, John's divorce attorney suggested he give *incentives* to other attorneys in town to avoid Mattie's case. These incentives were called "retainer fees." The retainer fees resulted in their refusal to take any case that might be considered a conflict of interest. The biggest conflict of interest of all would be representing Mattie in her divorce.

Help finally came in the form of a short, dumpy man with a receding hairline. His suit and shirt were a little too tight. His clothes looked rumpled as though he slept in them some nights. He called himself a "misfit" among other attorneys. Laughing, he stated a simple truth. "I'm honest."

In disbelief Mattie asked him, "So you'll take my case?"

He said, "Yes, I can't be bought off."

Mattie let out a relieved sigh and exclaimed "Thank you, God. Thank you for me and my daughter." Blinking back tears she looked at me and then looked heavenward, so the tears would not spill down onto her cheeks. Mattie never wanted me to see her cry.

I sat in the lobby with the receptionist coloring in a coloring book while Mattie and our new attorney talked.

The attorney carefully explained to Mattie exactly what was going on. My Father wanted a divorce that included getting the house, the car, and the bank accounts. The attorney explained the ultimate prize was me. John alleged had proof she was an unfit mother.

Mattie knew John was playing psychological games. He knew my brother Robert was taken away from her after her divorce from her previous husband, Robert, Sr. Mattie's only son; Robert Jr. was taken away while she looked for work. The arrangement was as soon as she found a suitable job, she would return to get her son back. However, her in-laws decided they did not want to give him up. Being without her son was an agonizing part of her life. They were apart until Robert was 16 years old. Mattie felt a pain in her gut as all those memories came flooding back like a tidal wave. How could he do this to me? What made him turn into this malicious animal, she wondered.

The attorney told Mattie no one parent had custody of me at this point. He told her, he thought John might make a kidnapping attempt. Back then, legally it wasn't considered kidnapping because there was no custody order, not even a temporary one. John could legally take me at any time. He could even leave town with me, he had that right. Mattie knew he had very close ties with his family in Texas. His tight-knit, well-to-do family wouldn't hesitate to go along with his plans.

Our attorney went to court to get an emergency temporary custody order. That was met with resistance from my John's attorney. He threatened to drag their dirty laundry into court sooner rather than later. Their plans were to file divorce papers based on charges of mental cruelty.

According to John's attorney, they had evidence that would prove Mattie was mentally unstable, an unfit parent and needed to be institutionalized. The judge ordered both parties back to court at another date.

Immediately, Mattie contacted my brother, Robert. A family meeting was called. These meeting generally included Mattie, my brother, and a host of male cousins. The male cousins were the same age as Robert. In their 30s, they called themselves "running buddies." The group concocted an elaborate plan of action regarding how to safeguard me.

They decided it was necessary to have someone with me at all times. Thus began my 'captivity'. I was to be dropped off and picked up from school every day. The school was given instructions who all were allowed to pick me up at the end of the school day. The person who picked me up had to get out of the car and I identify them as a person on the list. No pick-up was permitted otherwise. Then, I would stay at Robert and Audrey's house until Mattie got home from work. She would pick me up, and then next we would go to our temporary "home" for the evening. The temporary home was either Aunt Willie Mae's, or, some evenings we remained at my brother's house.

My niece, Wilma, and I attended the neighborhood Catholic School. Before the plan was put in place, I normally walked from school to her house, about three blocks away. Now, I had to wait outside beside a Nun, assigned pick-up duty for the day.

You know that uneasy feeling you get when you are in trouble and the teacher is waiting with you to talk to your parents? That's how I felt after school every day. Fellow students looked at me with accusing eyes. They believed something was wrong. Why else would a Nun, an authority figure, be standing there waiting for someone to pick me up? It wasn't what they thought. I was not allowed to tell anyone why I had to wait to be picked up. At six years old, I didn't quite understand it myself. My niece, Wilma, could walk home, or, wait along with me for my ride. Typically, she walked home with her neighborhood friends. There I stood waiting.

When the overseer arrived and got out of the car according to plan, the Nun would ask me if that was the right person.

I responded, "Yes" and off I went, typically for a three block ride.

I could not play outside with other children unless an adult, assigned to oversee me, was available to watch.

Eventually, word got out in the neighborhood what was really happening. There was a lot of gossip between adults and kids eavesdropped. The neighborhood kids wanted to help protect me from harm. Their intentions were pure, but my feelings were crushed when they called John names like 'evil'.

John owned a rental house across the street from my brother's house. One Saturday as my niece and I were playing in her room, we heard a commotion outside. Wilma and I ran to the screen door and saw John's rental house was burning. The flames were so intense, so powerful we could feel the heat from across the street and inside the screen door. By the time the Fire Department arrived, the house was fully engulfed.

John finally arrived to survey the damage as the Fire Department worked trying to extinguish the flames. I had not seen him in months.

My heart was pounding, "Daddy!" I shouted, but he could not hear me. The noise from the inferno and the Fire Department equipment overpowered my voice. He looked sad at the loss of the rental home. I wanted to run across the street and give him a hug but of course I could not do that. I felt empty inside. Although I knew John could do ugly things, he was still my Dad and I loved him. There was no doubt in my mind he loved me and wanted to see me, too. I was afraid to tell Wilma how I felt. I just knew she would question how I could love someone 'so evil'.

I talked with Mattie about it. She was such an understanding woman. She explained to me she feared a possible kidnapping attempt by John.

Mattie said, "You're so special we both want custody of you."

I asked, "Why can't you and daddy share?"

She explained she was trying really hard to have a plan for sharing. Gently she said, "I know this is hard on you and I hope it will be over soon." She also thanked me for being a great daughter.

Mattie started to believe someone was following her. Unnerving incidents occurred. The most obvious sign was an unfamiliar car parked on our street from time to time. We had moved into a tiny attic apartment she thought John didn't know about. One evening after dark, Mattie needed to use the phone. Back in 1963, if you didn't have a home phone, the only phone available was a pay phone. The one nearest to us was located on a pole half a block away from our apartment. Mattie grabbed me by the hand and up the street we walked. In the distance we saw a dark car, with an amber colored light glowing inside. As we grew closer to the car the light went out.

Mattie panicked, "Stop! We gotta go back!" We turned and ran back to our apartment. Shaking, she fumbled with the keys "Oh God. Oh God!" her voice trembled. Finally, we were safe in our little apartment again. Mattie was never certain if she simply over-reacted or if there was something to genuinely be concerned about.

By this time Mattie had graduated from Cosmetology School. She was working long hours at a local salon trying to establish her customer base. After work we sometimes stopped at Kroger's, the neighborhood grocery store. One day we were inside the store just a few minutes when Mattie started acting strange. She grabbed my hand so tight I cried, "Ouch!"

We went up one aisle and down another without picking a single item.

I asked her, "Mom, what's going on?"

She replied, "Shhhh!" as we bolted for the store exit picking up speed with every step. We were in a fast trot by the time we reached the car across the parking lot. Mattie didn't bother opening the passenger door for me to get in. She just shoved me in the driver's side door in full panic mode.

I kept asking, "Mom, what's wrong?"

She said she was not sure yet. On the drive home Mattie was quiet, frequently looking out the rearview mirror.

Mattie consulted with her attorney the next day. He said he would investigate, but in the meantime she should document everything. He told her she had good instincts and to follow them. He also told her she should consider staying with someone she trusted.

Mattie was known to be incredibly headstrong and refused to move from our little attic apartment. We divide our time between my brother Robert's, my aunt Willie Mae's, and our tiny, attic apartment.

Usually I fell asleep in the car before we arrived home because Mattie worked late into the night. One evening as I slept in the back seat, I was suddenly jolted awake by a sharp turn that nearly sent me to the car floorboard.

I called out, "What's going on?"

"Hang on!" She replied

"Why? What's going on?" I kept asking

She said, "Someone is following us."

I wanted to cry. But I kept my tears inside and held on for dear life. I swayed in the backseat as she made sharp turns first left, then right. I thought it would never end. Finally, she said she did not see him anymore. It was over and we were home at our apartment once again.

Mattie's attorney informed her, yes; John and his attorney had in fact hired a Private Investigator. In those days the person who filed for divorce needed to have a valid reason for filing. No-fault divorce laws were still years away. The Private Investigator's job was to uncover any dark secrets Mattie might have proving she was at fault in the dissolution of the marriage.

Was she having an affair? No, so the only scenarios in John's mind revolved around Mattie's mental state. They wanted to prove she was incapable of taking care of a husband and child. Not only did he want to show she was at fault, he also wanted full custody of me. Also, John and his family wanted Mattie away from any of the family money.

If the goal of the PI was not to tip Mattie off, he had done a poor job. He trailed her every day, everywhere she went. She knew it. After learning from her attorney that indeed John had hired a Private Investigator; Mattie was ready for battle.

Anytime we were followed, Mattie would go into, *James Bond mode*. Her goal was to lose her *tail*. She actually seemed to enjoy the challenge of evading him. Over time, I became an expert *spotter*. Any time our car made any unusual moves I woke up in the back seat. I felt like James Bond's helper looking out the rear window, letting her know if we had lost our tail.

It seemed like everywhere we went the PI was there taking pictures. Mattie would get hang-up calls at the hair salon where she worked. My brother Robert and his wife Audrey would get calls asking for his mother. Robert and Audrey frequently received wrong number calls and hang-up calls.

40

My parents finally returned to court to resolve the temporary custody issue.

John's attorney said Mattie was mentally ill and she could not take care of a child, therefore he should have full custody.

The judge immediately asked for proof of her mental frailty as documented from a medical professional.

The attorney could only produce a couple of flimsy affidavits signed by people he knew. The judge ruled that there was no medical proof and the argument was invalid. Divorce for reasons of mental instability or mental illness was frequently attempted back in those days, because someone had to be at fault for a divorce to be granted.

The judge stated he must have substantial proof that could be used at the time of the divorce hearing.

Our rumpled, honest attorney told the Judge his client, Mattie, was being harassed. He presented the journal of information Mattie carefully documented over the months. The Judge agreed it amounted to harassment, but the Private Investigator was merely doing his job. The Judge decided Mattie should get temporary custody of me with weekly visitations with John. Despite the fears Mattie's attorney voiced to the judge about possible kidnapping, the Judge held firm. Her attorney asked for third party to be present during visits with John. The judge did not feel it was necessary and held firm on his decision. No third party needs to be present during shared custody visits with John.

Mattie's attorney feared John may have undue influence with the Judge. He had no choice but to agree to visitation every weekend from 8:00 am on Saturday to 8:00 pm Sunday.

No one in the family was comfortable with John seeing me alone. Once again, a family meeting was held. This time, family members would act as Private Investigators to make sure they knew where I was at all times during visitations with John.

Visits with John were always at his house. My room was still the way I left it minus a few cherished toys I took with me when I fled with Mattie. My time was spent mostly in that room playing alone. The only time I remember coming out was for meals. I did not have a close relationship with him. Looking back now, I believe he truly did not know how to cultivate one.

I'm not sure if John realized it, a male family member was always parked within view the entire time. The cousins worked in shifts.

Mattie's attorney's qualms about undue influence with the Judge seemed be true. Each time there was a court date; John's attorney would have an excuse to get one extension after another.

Finally, the day of my parent's trial arrived. After two and a half years of negotiations, non-negotiations, conferences, and motions they still had not reached an agreement. Mattie told me the first miracle came with a new Judge. The Judge who presided over all the previous court dates was out on medical leave. John's "paid off" judge would have no power to give him everything in the settlement. The situation changed completely to her favor despite all the money thrown around to attorneys and the presiding judge. Mattie always considered it part of the "magic" that in the final throes of the divorce a new judge was assigned to the case.

Mattie and her attorney came armed with documentation and character witnesses. John and his attorney brought intimidating volumes of documents they thought would persuade the Judge in their favor. Strangely enough he had no character witnesses to call to the bench, just the Private

Investigator. The judge started off asking about the settlement of property and money issues. Mattie only wanted my bedroom furniture, all her clothes, and, the furniture from the spare bedroom. John, through his attorney, said she didn't deserve anything but her clothes. She was abusive to him even causing him physical harm.

The Judge immediately asked John and his attorney, "Any documented proof or witnesses?"

"We thought we had a witness, but she decided not to testify," John's attorney responded.

"So, no real documented proof exists either," the Judge countered.

Next the Judge asked about child custody arrangements.

John said he wanted full custody. He lied, and claimed Mattie had a boyfriend she lived with, and, I was there also, in a tiny apartment. John continued, "She makes little money and works long hours, resulting in late nights for me. That wasn't a good way to raise a child," he said. "I have plenty of money and can provide a nice home, the home my daughter was born in. Also, I will be retiring soon and will have plenty of time." John fought like a madman for full custody. He grasped at every possible straw, trying to prove my Mattie was unfit to raise a child.

Mattie also asked for full custody. Her attorney presented her character witnesses. Some of the witnesses saw the PI harassing Mattie with me present outside the grocery store. The landlord of the apartment Mattie rented was also present. He claimed Mattie and I were always together. Mattie told the Judge about all the abuse, both mentally and physically. The PI harassing her was just an extension of the ongoing psychological abuse in the marriage.

Fortunately, the Judge saw right through John's lies and arrogance. He came across as highly offensive and the Judge let him know it. He awarded Mattie both full custody and child support.

John had run up mountain of legal fees in the divorce and it was about to get even worse. The judge also ordered John to pay all of Mattie's legal bills. Finally, the Judge awarded her the furniture and the clothes she requested.

I was at my brother Robert's house when Mattie finally returned from the courthouse. She practically ran into the house. With one big swoop she scooped me up into her arms and joyfully said, "You're all mine now. It's just you and me against the world! And yes baby, you can see your daddy."

★　　★　　★

Life Lessons

I believe divorce is harder on the children than it is on adults. In high-conflict violent marriages, children like me benefit from divorce. Although I wanted my parents to separate, their divorce really shook my personal universe.

Children of divorced parents are forced to enter an adult world of responsibilities and worries at a young age. I was forced to deal with the conflicts and criticisms between my parents. At one point, I was caught in the middle, a prisoner of the circumstances. Everything I did and everywhere I went had to be monitored. I could not walk home from school or play outside freely like other children. Children are not like property that can be divided; they need love, stability and moral guidance.

Back when my parents divorced, times were quite different. Couples generally felt it was their obligation to stay together. In the 1960s, divorcing couples had to prove legal grounds to be granted a divorce. These grounds were typically desertion, abandonment, cruelty, or adultery. In order to prove legal grounds one spouse typically hired a Private Investigator. So, hiring Private Investigators or PIs was a common practice. Today, no-fault divorce laws usually make the process far less malicious.

Make Divorce Your Last Resort: All marriages have good and bad times. Marriage is an emotional roller coaster as are all relationships. When you marry the one you love, you assume these conditions, along with the responsibilities. Your vows state "for better for worse." In the bad times, many people decide to abandon ship and the relationship.

Every marriage has hope. You need to carefully think things through, especially if you have kids. If you decide to give it another shot, take a serious look at everything.

Take a good look at yourself, your spouse, the marriage and try to figure out exactly what is wrong. Is it financial pressure, or many little things gone wrong? There are many steps you can take to improve your marriage. Together stop and evaluate while you still can. Take a strong look at the problems. Once you identify your problems, address them slowly one by one.

If You Must Divorce, Make it Amicable: Divorce is never painless. If you and your spouse make an effort to distance yourself from your hurt, angry feelings, you can actually have an *amicable divorce*. Divorce does not have to always mean animosity and dirty tricks. Try to stay level-headed. Approach your divorce with the respect for the relationship you once had. This is especially true when you have children. A friendly divorce will help your children heal more quickly from the breakup of the family.

Try your best to keep the channels of communication open. Once you decide to open the lines of communication, decide on a time and place to discuss your divorce. Use the meeting to discuss everything from finances to visitation if you have children.

Always opt for *collaborative* instead of *adversarial* litigation. If you cannot come to agreement on issues like alimony or child custody, there are legal options such as mediation available. In mediation, a Mediator trained in conflict resolution will facilitate the conversations between you and your estranged spouse.

The largest cost in most divorces is usually the retainer paid to your divorce lawyer. The more you and your spouse can work things out together, the less expensive these attorney fees will be for both of you.

Hostility: If your best attempts at an amicable divorce have failed, be aware of dirty tricks your former spouse may try to play on you. Divorce often starts out amicably and gradually becomes nasty in the hands of those people who choose to play power games. Watch out for angry, vindictive soon-to-be ex-spouses who feel they must win at all costs.

What to do if it happens in your divorce: There are several ways to prepare for and manage your divorce. First, recognize a schemer and a power player. Second, do not lose your cool or try to fight fire with fire. It will only escalate the problem, and, your family will suffer as a result. Finally, think ahead and plan positive steps to counter the power game.

- ☐ Always use an attorney with experience and knowledge of divorce and family law so your interests are protected.

- ☐ Be honest and up front with your attorney. Make sure to fully disclose all your assets and property to him or her.

- ☐ Try to be flexible with your spouse. Doing your best to find a middle ground often results in a quicker, easier divorce process.

- ☐ Always document everything. Keep a journal of important dates and events.

- ☐ Remember to pick your battles carefully. Use good, solid business sense when deciding what to fight for and at what cost. It is ridiculous to spend thousands of dollars in attorney fees fighting for a $200 piece of furniture.

- ☐ Never pull money out of jointly held bank accounts; put everything into an account in your name alone.

- ☐ Do not use credit cards to purchase and stock up on personal items, or, make large purchases at this time.

- ☐ Getting greedy will cost you in unnecessary attorney fees.

☐ Well-meaning friends telling you what to do are usually not your best source of advice and information. Their intentions are good. However, listen to your attorney. Attorneys know the law.

When it comes to your children it's important that they feel as secure as possible even in the midst of a divorce. Never discuss the details of the divorce with your children. Do not put your children in the middle. You should never put your spouse down or say mean-spirited things about him in front of the children. After all, he is still their father.

Do not use your children as a bargaining chip or as a pawn. Never stop your children from seeing their other parent during regular visitations because he or she owes you money, unless there truly is a possibility the other parent might abuse the child in some way. It's tempting, but it will only damage the relationship further.

Divorce is never easy for anyone involved. It typically has a long-term effect on future relationships for both you and your children as they become adults. You may feel insecure, betrayed and suffer from feelings of low self-esteem long after your divorce is over. It's not uncommon to feel anger, sadness, depression, and frightened about your future.

Try your best to make your divorce a learning experience. Look at it as an opportunity to make yourself stronger and healthier emotionally as a person. Focus on the positive aspects still in your life. It may not seem like it right now, but people do heal from divorce. Look to the future and picture a happier you.

Your happiness all depends on your attitude. Believe!

★　　　★　　　★

BROKEN

"The journey may be long. The pain can be overwhelming. Stand and walk the path to healing. Peace will come and the brokenness will no longer be." —Author Unknown

Three years after Mattie left her mother's home at the age of 12, she married a local boy named Robert Williams. Soon after the wedding she was pregnant. Nine months later she gave birth to her first child Robert Williams, Jr. at the age of 15 on September 15, 1929. Her marriage to Robert Sr. was short lived. After one and a half years they were divorced. As a divorced mother at only 16 years old back in 1930, Mattie agreed to let Robert Sr.'s family take care of my brother Robert Jr. until she found suitable work.

After six months, Mattie found a good job as a housekeeper with a wealthy couple. They agreed it would be alright for her to bring her baby son to live together with her. Mattie sent a letter to her in-laws sharing her good news. Their response shocked Mattie. Her in-laws decided they wanted to raise Robert, Jr. She was told she could visit him whenever she wanted.

Mattie tried over the years to get her son back, to no avail. When my brother Robert Jr. turned 16, he was able to legally proclaim his independence from his father's family. He was tired of being kept away from his mother and was ready to live with her in Kansas City. Finally, mother and son were reunited. Mattie was overjoyed and very proud to have her son back.

At age 19 my brother Robert was drafted into the military. He only served one year in the Korean War. In 1950 he returned home to his mother. He had seen battle; however, he suffered no injuries and was safe and sound.

Later, Robert found his soul mate, Audrey. They got married and their union produced a daughter, Wilma.

<hr />

Fast forward to 1964 when my parents' divorce was final

That day, the second she got to my brother's home, in one big swoop she lifted me in the air, spun me around, and announced, "You're all mine!" Everything appeared right with the world after her returned from the last divorce court hearing. The divorce was granted and custody for me was established. Mattie was ecstatic and at peace again.

Everything was about to change for the worse.

The court granted Mattie my bedroom furniture, all her clothes, and the furniture from the spare bedroom. She was given 30 days to retrieve these items. Arrangements were made through her attorney to pick up all items listed in the divorce decree for two weeks from that court date. As the day got closer John reneged on the arrangement.

There was always an excuse. Thirty days turned into sixty. And sixty turned into ninety. My brother and other family members became incensed at his foot-dragging. The situation grew intense. Family members talked of going to John's house and taking everything they could and sort it all out later. Mattie tried to diffuse the situation opting to take the legal route instead.

As a result, Mattie and her attorney had to go back to court and demand a date to retrieve the items that were awarded her.

$\sim\!\!\star\!\!\sim\!\!\sim\!\!\sim\!\!\star\!\!\sim\!\!\sim\!\!\sim\!\!\star\!\!\sim$

September 16th

The day finally arrived. By that time Mattie had been dating a man named Collier for about three months. My brother, Robert, rented a U-Haul truck. Mattie's boyfriend Collier drove it with our cousin Jason riding along. Robert, along with our cousins George, James, Mattie and I rode in the car. They dropped me off at my cousin Mildred's house to play. Mildred's children and I were around the same age. Robert said, "See you later, Squirt." Those were the last words I ever heard him speak.

After the group arrived, Collier stayed inside the truck while Mattie, my brother, and cousins went on the porch. John only allowed Mattie into the house.

"Whatever you gonna get, you have to get it to the door yourself," John shouted angrily.

My cousins tried to reason with him. No luck.

"She can't get that furniture down the stairs by herself, man!" One by one they pleaded with John to be let inside the house.

Mattie tried to calm the situation. "It's okay, I'll bring down what I can for now," she said. She was hoping if things went smoothly with the small items he would finally allow my brother and cousins to come in and get the four heaviest furniture pieces.

As she made one more trip down the two flights of stairs, Mattie was exhausted. Everything appeared to be going smoothly. As John entered the foyer, Mattie asked if he would reconsider letting family members come in to help move the heaviest pieces.

"I told you already. Whatever you gonna get, you have to get it to the door yourself!" he shouted at her.

"That court didn't say I had to let anyone inside but you," John taunted her with a sarcastic tone.

My brother was beside himself. By this point he'd had it. The years of dragging his mother through the living hell of this divorce and the custody battle for me all came to a head. He started a yelling match at John.

John told everyone to get off the porch.

Robert shouted, "No!"

Jason just stood there. Collier stayed near the street next to the U-Haul. Again, Mattie tried to calm the situation. Without a word, John turned and went up the stairs.

Mattie said she would get what she could. She asked everyone to please wait on the sidewalk. She talked with Robert, her beloved son for a few minutes before turning to go back up the stairs. Mattie assumed Robert and the cousins would wait on the sidewalk as instructed.

She went upstairs for another trip as John was coming down. No words were spoken as they passed each other on the staircase.

When Mattie reached the top of the stairs, she heard a single gunshot ring out in the clear afternoon air. Instantly, Mattie turned and ran down the stairs. She screamed in terror as she found her baby boy lying on the porch in a puddle of blood. She saw one bullet hole above his left eye.

"My baby, my baby! Somebody help my baby!" Mattie cried out in anguish

"How could you hurt my baby?" she yelled at John.

John stood frozen in place, the gun still in his grasp. He did not answer. He did not get help. It was as if he lost all sense of reality.

Mattie cradled her baby, Robert. As she lifted him, a gun fell out of the waistband of his trousers. Later she told me she took his gun and hid it in her brassiere. She held him and talked to him until an ambulance arrived. When the shot was fired my cousins ran in different directions. Robert was the only person that day who refused to leave John's porch.

When he reached the hospital Robert was still alive. The doctors told Mattie he had a slim chance to make it. If he did, he would be "a vegetable" the rest of his life. He died later that evening, just one day after his 35th birthday. Everyone's life change that day.

How do you tell a seven-year-old girl her only brother, her only sibling was dead at the hands of her father?

At my cousin Mildred's house I played until it grew dark outside. I wondered what was taking so long. I felt sleepy and tired. I just wanted to go home. My cousin Mildred said it would be awhile and to just sleep on the sofa.

When Mattie finally arrived it was very late at night. Or, maybe it was already the early morning hours. Just Mattie and Collier came to pick me up. As soon as we got in the car my first question was, "Mom where is brother?"

After a long pause she said, "He'll be home later."

I was too tired and sleepy to drill them on his whereabouts.

Instead of going to our house we went to Robert's house. As Mattie, Collier and I walked up the driveway, Mattie stopped dead in her tracks. She let out a loud scream and started crying. The pain of her dead son was just too much to bear. She could not hold in her grief any longer. I asked her what was wrong. She didn't respond and instead just buried her head in Collier's chest.

Once inside I jumped in the bed my niece Wilma and I used to share and fell asleep. The next morning I awoke to a house full of people. I searched for Robert but still could not find him. I was frustrated. No one would tell me where he was. I found Mattie and noticed her eyes were still puffy and red from crying.

I asked again, "Where is brother?" I wondered why there were so many people in the house.

She took me by the hand and led me to the bedroom in the back of the house. Then she closed the door. We were alone in that house full of people.

We were both sitting on the bed facing each other when she finally began to speak. "I have some very bad news." She told me. "Your brother was hurt very bad," she said. Mattie's voice broke with emotion and sorrow.

I had so many questions. "Is he in the hospital? I want to see him. How did he get hurt?"

Mattie told me John hurt him very bad with a gun yesterday and Robert died.

I started to scream and cry. "I don't understand. I want to see my brother," I wailed. I yanked open the bedroom door and ran for the front of the house. Someone caught me before I could get out the front door. I started kicking and screaming. Mattie grabbed me, held me and carried me back to the bedroom. We both just cried and held on to each other. I cried myself back to sleep. When I woke up I heard family and neighbors talking in the house. I didn't want to come out of the small bedroom.

The story surrounding Robert's death quickly reached the news media. Mattie asked my brother's best friend, Alvin Brooks, to speak for the family. She kept checking in on me. I think I was keeping her as sane as possible through this tragic time.

Mattie contacted Robert's wife Audrey "Sis" who was in Houston at the time. She only told her and my niece Wilma to come back to Kansas City. Mattie never told Sis why. Of course she knew it had to be bad news. Back then, people avoided giving news of the death of a loved one over the telephone whenever possible.

The days leading up to Robert's funeral were very difficult. A doctor prescribed sedatives for Mattie so she would sleep more soundly. She struggled to make it through every second, every minute, and every hour of each agonizing day.

The family had awful things to say about John, including wanting to kill him for revenge.

Mattie never once said I should "hate my father" or "he is a terrible person". In fact, Mattie never uttered a negative word about John to me. She was incredibly stoic and strong. Actually, Mattie told me John said afterwards it was an accident. He just wanted to scare Robert away from the front porch with the gunshot. I think Mattie instinctively knew I was confused by it all. Whose side was I supposed to be on? I loved both my parents.

The entire family, including me, was simply numb throughout the wake, Catholic funeral rites, and the burial. Mattie was still sedated at the funeral.

Everyone was busy trying to help Mattie and Sis, before and after the funeral maybe a little too much. Finally, Mattie locked herself in the bedroom. We all survived in our own fog, but we were forever changed by that single gunshot that killed my brother Robert.

Would John be charged with second degree murder?

John kept calling Sis on the phone. No one in the family wanted her to speak to him. One night John finally got through to Sis on the phone. He was sobbing uncontrollably begging for forgiveness. It was an accident he cried.

Sis told him she had already forgiven him. She said she could not live the rest of her life in a state of hate. My niece and her mother returned to Houston soon after.

The District Attorney was considering charging John with second degree murder. A week after the funeral, Mattie told me the police phoned her to ask if she wanted charges filed against John. If Mattie did that, it meant he would go to prison. She asked how I felt about it.

I told her, "Mommy it won't bring brother back."

In the end she didn't file charges against John. So, the police didn't file charges, either.

I was seven years old when my brother died. Now I'm in my fifties. I have never seen the court (or police) records. When I'm feeling courageous enough, I want to know all that happened that tragic day. John never told me why the District Attorney didn't filed charges, either. The rumors and gossip mill said charges were never filed because Robert was on John's property, and he told him clearly to get off his property.

The magic is this tragedy was that Mattie still had a daughter. Mattie question God when she became pregnant with me. Why Lord why so late in life? She would question the Creator. He knew she would be losing her son that's why. Mattie knew she had a young daughter to live for.

✮　　✮　　✮

Life Lessons

The death of my brother could have been avoided. As parents, you cannot let a divorce be all consuming. Were the material possessions Mattie came to get from John's house important enough to risk a dangerous situation? Why did John think losing some material possessions important enough to use a gun? This became a battle of wills. It was more about the principle of the matter, right or wrong, than the replaceable items in the house.

After Robert's death, Mattie was never completely the same. She never got over it, and, of course she blamed herself. Mattie felt so much pain and guilt for the death of her child. I wished she had a healthy way to deal with her pain. It would have been helpful for her to talk to a therapist or counselor. However, that was unheard of in 1964; people in the African-American community never talked with a therapist. Back then, the church leaders were the only source of counseling. They were not trained counselors. They could only instruct the faithful to stay strong and pray. The African-American community believed if the church couldn't help you, no one could.

Mattie's wound from her sons' death never healed. It stayed below the surface until something painful would crack the wound open once again.

Our family and friends continued to love her and did all they could to be supportive. Mattie was always the strong one in the family. It was hard for her to be the vulnerable one and reach out to others. She needed to know asking for help was not a sign of weakness but of strength.

Mattie's grief, or the grief of any parent who loses a child, is a lifetime journey. A bereaving parent experiences the most intense sadness known to humankind. When a child dies, the parents feel a part of them has died and their soul has been ripped away.

Today there are many support systems for family members that can help. These systems were not in place when my brother Robert died.

Turn to friends and family members: Now is the time to lean on the people who care about you. Let them in, even if you take pride in being strong. Don't avoid loved ones. Draw them near. Accept the assistance that's offered to you. Often, people want to help someone who is grieving, but they simply don't know how. So, tell them what you need whether it's a shoulder to cry on, or help with funeral arrangements.

Draw comfort from your faith: If you follow a religious tradition, embrace the comfort it can provide you during this difficult time. Spiritual activities that are meaningful to you, like praying, meditating, or going to church can offer comfort. If you're questioning your faith, talk to a clergy member.

Join a support group: Grief can feel very lonely, even when you have loved ones near. Sharing your sorrow with others who have experienced similar losses can help. Find a bereavement support group in your area. Your local hospitals, hospices, funeral homes, and counseling centers can point you in the right direction.

Talk to a therapist or grief counselor: If your grief feels like too much to bear, call a mental health professional with experience in grief counseling. An experienced therapist can help you work through your intense emotions and help you overcome the obstacles to your grieving.

☆　　☆　　☆

LOVE BANDIT

"Some true love turned and not a false turned true."
—William Shakespeare

After years of physical and psychological abuse in her relationships with men, Mattie finally found her knight in shining armor. Or so she thought.

Her *knight* was Collier, a chauffeur for the wealthy owner of a local lumber company. Mattie met him when she was separated, originally about a year before her divorce from John was finalized. They started officially dating three months before my brother died. Though they did not live together at the beginning, he was ever-present in her life. He was a comforting, reassuring shoulder for Mattie to cry on, and, a sounding board on which to bounce ideas. He was also generous with gifts he gave both Mattie and me.

My brother, Robert, of course never trusted Collier. Mattie ignored my brother's concerns. She believed in his eyes no one would ever be good enough for his momma. So, she ignored his warnings. After all, when she met Collier it had been a very long time since she had a kind, considerate man in her life.

Mattie's considerate, knight in shining armor, was the man driving the U-Haul on September 16, 1964 that fateful day when my brother was killed. When the argument between Robert and John heated up, as the shot rang out, Collier hid behind a tree in the yard.

Collier was at the hospital when Robert passed away from that single gunshot wound. He continued supporting Mattie throughout the funeral and in her grief. He told her everything she wanted to hear.

About nine months after Robert's death, Mattie married Collier. I had just finished spending the summer in Houston, Texas with family. When I arrived back home to Kansas City, he had moved in and they were legally married. Mattie appeared very happy with this arrangement.

That fall I started third grade in a public school, for the first time, with a new last name. To the outside world we appeared as one big, happy family. I knew Mattie was doing her best trying to create a normal family for me. We had both been through so much over the last few years from abuse, divorce, to Robert's death. The truth is I never really connected with Collier; but I stayed quiet.

I was not going for visitations with John at the time. The courts left it up to Mattie to decide on a visitation schedule if and when she was ready. Collier didn't think it was a good idea for me to have any contact with John. Mattie was still debating the issue, but for the first time she didn't ask me what I wanted. That was different from the mom I knew.

I wanted to see John. I wanted to ask him, "Daddy what happened between you and brother?" Maybe I didn't want to ask him at all. I just wanted to see him. I was never asked.

Mattie was a changed woman. She still gave love, but she was certainly not the same person she was before. For the first time there seemed to be a disconnect between Mattie and me. She seemed happy with her life on the surface. For the entire world to see, she had survived and moved on after repeated tragedies. People saw Mattie Fisher as a tower of strength. However, when I looked in her eyes they seemed dead to me.

Mid-way through third grade strange things started happening at our home. I didn't really understand what was happening at the time.

Collier was gone some nights. Mattie always told me he was working. Mrs. D., Collier's employer, needed to go somewhere or do something. He said he was too tired to drive back home. Sometimes Mrs. D. needed to be driven out of town because she was afraid to fly. He would be gone several days at a time. When Collier was home there seemed to be fights between he and Mattie about money missing from their bank account.

When Mattie started to grow suspicious of Collier and his spending habits, he turned to another source for cash Mrs. D. Apparently Mrs. D. was always willing to help Collier out with cash. Collier was always reliable, and he felt like a family member after Mrs. D's husband died.

One time Collier told Mrs. D. I broke my arm and we needed money for the hospital bill. Mrs. D. gave him $300 to take care of 'medical expenses'. A couple days later Mrs. D. called the house and Mattie answered the phone. Mrs. D. asked to speak to Collier to see if he was available to drive her to a special event she wanted to attend.

Making pleasant conversation she first asked Mattie, "How is the baby?"

Mattie replied, "Fine, she's outside in the yard playing."

"So how long will she be in that cast?" Mrs. D. asked with concern.

"What cast?" Mattie was confused.

Mrs. D. told Mattie the whole story as it was relayed to her by Collier. Mattie stuttered, as she tried to fully understand what was happening.

"How much did he borrow from you Mrs. D.?"

"Oh, he didn't borrow it. I told him he could have the $300." Mrs. D. repeated.

According to her, he had asked for and received money from her many times, for many things over the years. Mattie was speechless.

Gathering her thoughts, Mattie simply replied, "He's not here right now, but I will get to the bottom of all of this."

When Collier returned to the house Mattie confronted him. "Mrs. D. called today to see how D'Nita's arm was healing up." Collier came up with several versions of why he lied and asked his boss for money. Mattie's favorite version involved him buying her a gift for her birthday three months away. Of course, she wasn't buying any of it.

Mattie seemed to have let it go, but one look in her eyes and I felt my ol' feisty, sharp as a tack Mattie was finally back again. I just knew Mattie was casting her nets and setting up her "covert operations" and getting into detective mode again to find out the real answers to this caper.

Finally, Mattie discovered the answers she was searching for, but they certainly did not make her any happier. Collier had another family. Though he was not married, he had children with another woman. He was leading a double life. The nights and days he said he was working he was with his second family. His mistress knew full well about Mattie and me. He and his mistress were a team. They were con artists who prey on vulnerable women. Mattie was just his latest victim.

The end result? Collier, the man who supported Mattie through all her agonizing trials and tribulations was a 'love bandit con artist'. Even though Mattie had little money to begin with, he knew she was an entrepreneur. At that time she had a thriving salon business, and he knew she was going to get some type of divorce settlement from John. On top of that, she had her heart set on moving to a new home. He knew his patience would eventually pay off.

Once the gig was up, Collier let Mattie know he had no intention leaving the marriage empty-handed. He didn't care his name was not on the deed to the house, he still wanted his share. The house in Vineyard Woods she worked so hard to buy for us was in serious jeopardy.

The mother I knew my entire life was finally back.

Mattie was gradually developing a renewed relationship with her father, Oscar. Over a couple years she had grown to trust his wisdom and counsel. So, she called her father first. My grandfather worked out a temporary deal, and Oscar Fisher was named owner of our Vineyard Woods house. She always considered it *magical* the reason for Collier in her life is that it finally gave Mattie and her father an opportunity to grow very closer, since she lacked having a relationship with him growing up.

c⁓ා☆c⁓ාc⁓ා☆c⁓ාc⁓ා☆c⁓ා

When Mattie's divorce from Collier was finalized my last name was immediately changed back. She apologized, regretful for putting me through more drama.

"It's okay mommy, I know you were sad. You were just trying to make us happy again," I reassured her.

Family legend has it that my cousins, who vowed to take care of their Aunt Mattie after Robert's death, made a little deal of their own with Collier. Once his no-good intentions were clear and knowing my cousins as I do, I am 100 percent sure this legend is correct. Mattie did not have to worry anymore. Let's just say that in true *Godfather Style*, they made him a life or death offer he could not refuse.

We were finally free of Collier.

★　　★　　★

Life Lessons

In her later years, Mattie admitted her suspicions about Collier early in their relationship. It was the small things that never seemed to add up. She did not trust him totally. She chalked up her suspicions to her trust issues after a bad marriage. Mattie pushed those feelings aside because she wanted so desperately to feel a sense of family and moved full speed ahead marrying Collier. So there we were Mattie, Collier and me one small happy family.

Mattie had gone through so much. She needed to put the pieces of her life back together and feel normal again after so many years of pain. Again, Mattie tried to prove she could keep moving forward. The problem was she was in a 'window of vulnerability' when she met Collier. As a result of her nasty divorce, and the tragic loss of my brother Robert, Mattie developed emotional wounds that ran very deep. This left her open and vulnerable, her typically sharp defense mechanisms were lacking.

Mattie was an expert at masking her pain. She seemed determined to prove to the world just how tough she was every day. As a result, she moved on, quickly jumping into a new relationship. She never gave herself a chance to heal from John's emotional and physical abuse. She also did not give herself time to assess the lessons from that relationship and learn from her mistakes, therefore setting herself up to be defenseless and befriended by a con artist.

Using Collier as a quick heartbreak mender, Mattie put herself in situations and in a relationship she would normally not be caught dead in. Collier knew Mattie was lonely with a strong desire for intimacy and support. He also knew despite her tough appearance to the outside world, deep inside she craved love and acceptance.

What I do, and recommend, is to take some 'down time' after a relationship breakup and proceed with caution.

Take Time for You: Get up every morning with the thought that you are rebuilding your life. That alone is a major accomplishment. Don't forget to reward yourself. Take some of the time and energy previously focused on your partnership to make you feel better. Get a massage. Read a book. Take a long bike ride. Get to know yourself again. You now have the freedom to explore yourself. Try new things and learn what makes *you* happy. Start your life over beginning today and realize all the opportunities available to you. Look for your goals in life and find out how to achieve them. Don't forget to celebrate living single.

Some solitude can be good for all of us as a time to reflect. In your reflection time also think about the role you played in the failure of your relationship. Ask yourself, how am I causing this or contributing to this? Consider your past relationship issues and learn from your mistakes. If you are responsible about learning from how you contributed, it will touch other spaces in your life. After you have taken a good look at the role you played in your divorce, use it as an awakening. Make happiness your primary concern no matter who is to blame. Remember, as long as you make it the other person's fault you remain a victim.

Don't rush into another relationship: Be careful to take some time to get yourself grounded again before trying to tackle another relationship. Many therapists recommend waiting at least a year to give you time to work through the issues associated with divorce before getting involved with someone else. Rebound relationships are never good for either person involved. It's very easy to succumb to your natural feelings of wanting to be loved and needed. However, getting into another relationship too quickly and for the wrong reasons can only make you feel worse in the long run.

After a divorce we tend to feel emotionally raw, confused, anxious, depressed and therefore vulnerable. In this state of vulnerability, and being driven by so many other feelings, the easiest way to dampen these emotions is to focus on another person. These relationships have little hope of lasting or leaving off where the last one ended.

When you are ready, ease back in to new relationships: Take a little longer than you normally would to get to know someone. Take time to enjoy the dates as you are learning about each other. Make not seeing each other all the time exciting. After all, absence does make the heart grow fonder. It takes at least a full year to really get to know someone. Use that time wisely. Realize your post-divorce relationship is probably transitional.

See him or her as they are and not as you would like them to be. When we are in a low place it's easy to put a high value on a person's potential. Expect, that's not who they truly are. Can you love them and accept them exactly as they are today? After all, anything less is not unconditionally loving.

Most women want to turn a man into a project. Women's magazines feed right into this feminine wish to change our men. That's why you see so many articles about how to make him more romantic, or how to get him to do more around the house. If you are dealing with a person who's an adult, he's fully formed. What you see is what you get. Honestly, the only things you can easily change about a man are his hair and his clothes.

Relax and enjoy getting to know the new person. Don't hurry or rush yourself. Make sure you understand him/her. Remember, you want to get to know this person well, understand his feelings for you, and his future goals and plans. This will help you decide whether you can fit well into his life. Only then begin to consider a permanent relationship.

Ask yourself do you know their best friend? What are their favorite books? What makes them laugh or cry? Are their religious beliefs and their political persuasions compatible with your own? Do they fight to win, or work through conflict and accept compromise? Have they been a good parent? Are they financially stable? Can you talk heart-to-heart? Do you enjoy being around their family?

Having sex before you really know someone can break your heart. Learn to say, "Not yet. It's too soon." Anyone can have sex, but love and a true relationship take time—and lots of it— to build. If you're looking for a serious relationship, having sex too soon can muddy the waters. It's common for men to assume if she's willing to do this so quickly with me, who else is she having sex with? It might sound old fashion in today's world but it's still true. Women are generally the "moral compass" in relationships. People don't feel special when sex happens too soon after meeting each other. The general rule is not to be sexual with someone until you really know them well. Make sure you are clear that you are not only sexually attracted to them, but you like them as well.

Of course, you want to make certain your new partner feels the same. Until you're sure this is a person and a situation you want to commit to its okay to say, "Not yet."

You can do it in a gentle way that keeps their ego intact. For example, say, "I'm really flattered. I want to take things to the next step, but to be honest with you I don't feel I'm ready for that at this early stage in our relationship.

Their response is a good barometer of how they would be as a partner or a spouse. Never settle for relationships with people who take things too personally or turn these kinds of important decisions into a power struggle.

★   ★   ★

Figure 1 Mattie Fisher

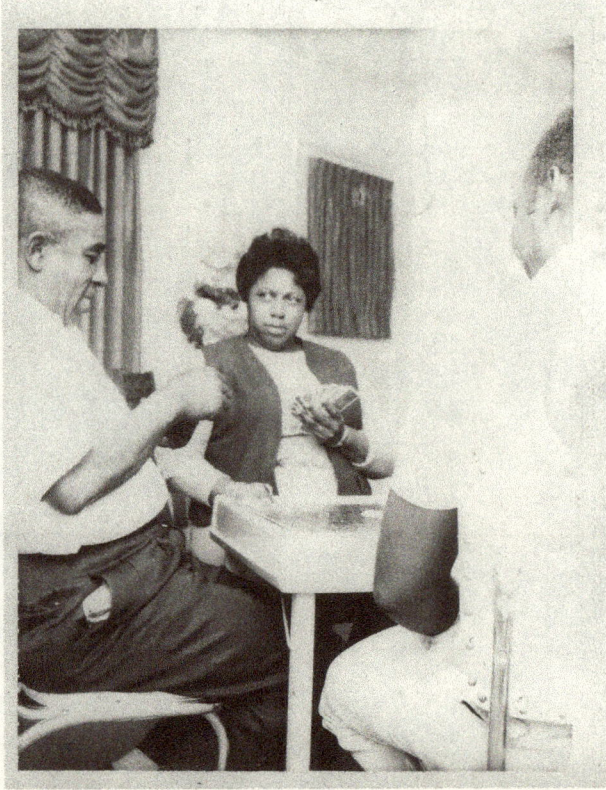

Figure 2 Giving Collier the 'look' - Mattie always knew

Figure 3 The last picture my dad gave me of himself

Figure 4 My handsome brother Robert in his Full-Dress Uniform

Figure 5 My brother Robert

Figure 6 Mom and Me

Figure 7 Dad, Grandma, and Cousin George

Figure 8 Mom, Audrey (Sis), and Dad

Figure 9 Mom, Me, and little Autumn (my daughter)

Figure 10 The Vineyard Woods house

THE SUPERNATURAL AND UNEXPLAINED

"There are an infinite number of universes existing side by side and through which our consciousness's constantly pass. In these universes, all possibilities exist. You are alive in some, long dead in others, and never existed in still others. Many of our 'ghosts' could indeed be visions of people going about their business in a parallel universe or another time—or both. —Paul F. Eno

Mattie was born a Caulbearer. The Caul or Face Veil is a thin, filmy membrane, the remnants of the amniotic sac that covers or partially covers a newborn's face immediately after birth. Some believe "Caul Children" have the ability to see behind the veil of life and death. It's thought they can communicate with the dead and intuitively 'know'. This was true for Mattie.

Mattie's family was shocked when she was born with her 'face veil'; it's rare. They knew what it meant to be a Caul Child, and they came to believe in the powers the she possessed.

Mattie never called herself a psychic or a medium. There were no séances or attempts to connect with the spiritual world and the great beyond. When Mattie saw or heard something unexplained it was always random and unprovoked.

Did she see dead people? Yes; sometimes she heard them, too. Mattie had a sixth sense. But that sixth sense can be fallible. It allows the person who is tuned into these frequencies to see only what is meant for them to see. Mattie taught me if we knew or were shown everything we would never learn anything. She always said, "We're here in this life to learn." It certainly created an interesting life for her—and for me.

There are many levels, planes and dimension to this life and the afterlife, Mattie explained to me. We all inhabit the same space, but each Spirit, physical and nonphysical remains distinct. Somehow the Creator makes each spiritual plane frequency unique and separate. This is so the inhabitants and activities of that frequency aren't disturbed by the many other beings inhabiting other frequencies. Every once in a while the frequencies cross. Her nonscientific explanations helped me understand when I heard voices in a room where no one else was physically present.

Mattie's first experience seeing the dead happened when she was only four years old. She was born to a very young unwed mother who could not fully take care of her, so her grandparents raised her. She lived with her grandparents on a farm with a lot of farm animals. Her greatest joy was a horse name Hosey. Her Grandpa let her ride the horse while he held on to the reins. She loved seeing her Grandpa sitting tall in the saddle riding Hosey. Each evening, right before dark, she stood at the large picture window overlooking the backyard. There she patiently waited for her Grandpa to come riding in on Hosey.

"He's here! He's here!" she would scream to her Grandma. Mattie would watch intently as Grandpa put Hosey to bed for the night. She tackled her Grandpa with big hugs every night as he came in the door. She loved to climb on his back for a pony ride into the kitchen.

One day she stood at the window until dark. "Grandpa and Hosey are really late Grandma," Mattie said. It had been a strange day filled with more people coming and going than usual. The *grown folk* seem to huddle and talk amongst themselves. Now the house was quiet.

After waiting for what seemed like forever Mattie ran to Grandma and asked, "Where is Grandpa and Hosey?"

"Your Grandpa's not coming back, Mattie Pearl," her Grandma slowly explained. "I think Hosey stepped on something and became off balance, throwing your Grandpa to the ground. He was injured very badly. That's why Mr. Ted and Mrs. Lilly came this morning. All the extra people were here to tell me they were sorry. I left with Mr. Ted to go see your Grandpa's body. I'm so sorry sweetie, Grandpa is dead."

"Where is Hosey?" Mattie probed.

"Hosey was hurt, too. They had to put him down," Grandma replied.

Mattie, five years old at the time, screamed and ran around the house. Her Grandma caught her and held her tightly, rocking back and forth in the chair. "It's okay baby we're going to be okay," she repeated, as if to convince herself.

Mattie was sent to stay with her own mother for few days. While she was gone a funeral wake was held at her Grandma's house followed by a burial on the farm grounds.

When she returned home, things seemed very different. Strangers were taking care of the farm and Grandma just didn't look the same. She felt hurt that she never got to say goodbye to her Grandpa. With tears in her eyes she stood at the window as the sun set just as she always did. As she turned to walk away she heard the galloping sounds of a horse. She looked up to see her Grandpa riding Hosey into the barn.

"He's here! He's here!" she screamed to her Grandma. "I knew he would come back!" She waited intently for Grandpa to come out of the barn. He didn't.

Precognition is defined as the knowledge of a future event or situation, especially through extrasensory means. Mattie's first experience with precognition, that she remembered, happened when she was six.

Mattie's grandparents and her mother lived within an hour walking distance from each other. After the death of her Grandpa she visited her mother, Mary, more often. Mattie loved the walk. The scenic views of daffodils, daisies, lush greenery and a clear blue stream meandered through the countryside along the way. She spent many days on the banks of that stream as her Grandma fished.

One late afternoon as Mattie and her Grandma walked to her mother Mary's house, they decided to take a shortcut through the woods by the stream. Mattie ran ahead wanting to pick flowers for her mother. While gathering flowers she looked up to see a woman walking at a perpendicular angle.

She wondered who the woman was.

As the woman grew near, she recognized it was her Grandma with a fishing pole. Mattie, age six at the time, stood in utter amazement. She looked behind her and there was her Grandma again without the fishing pole. How could this be?

Frozen, Mattie dropped the flowers she had picked. She stood there quietly as the two women continued walking toward one another on a collision path. Then it happened, they passed each other, neither one acknowledging the other. The woman with the fishing pole continued walking down to the stream.

"Grandma, why did that woman look like you?" Mattie asked in an animated voice.

"What woman?" Grandma asked.

"Grandma, you didn't see her? She walked right passed you with her fishing pole. She went down to the stream to fish. How could you not see her Grandma?" Mattie wanted Grandma to walk down the stream's bank with her to prove her point.

In a calm voice, Grandma softly said "No" to soothe Mattie's hysterics.

"Let's keep walking, we need to get to your mother's house before dark," Grandma said.

Mattie stubbornly stood there a few more minutes staring the direction where the mysterious woman walked.

They arrived at the house right before dark. Mary had since married and had two other kids with her husband. Mattie was shooed into the other room with her half siblings so the grown-ups could talk. Mattie had a feeling the conversation would be about the mystery woman with the fishing pole, so she stayed close by the room. Leaning close to the door, she listened intently.

Grandma finally said, "Mattie Pearl saw a spirit on the way over here. She said it looked just like me."

Mary, asked, "What does that mean, Momma?"

Before Mattie could overhear anything else, her half sibling let the grown-ups know she was listening in on their conversation. Mattie was reprimanded for disobeying an order and was sent to bed early.

The next day on the way back to her grandparents' house, Mattie and her Grandma took the longer way home. The entire time Mattie was looking for the mystery lady with the fishing pole but she never appeared again.

By the time they arrived back home her Grandma had developed a bad cough. She went to bed right away with some medicated salve on her chest.

The next morning Grandma seemed worse. Her skin was hot to the touch and she was not able to get out of bed without assistance. So she asked Mattie to call one of the farm helpers. The farm helper rode to the local Negro doctor for help. When the doctor finally arrived Grandma was heaving. Mattie scared, was crying in another room. The doctor asked the farm helper to go fetch Mary. Everything seemed chaotic all day long. Mary came out of her Grandma's bedroom to spend time with Mattie several times throughout the day.

Mattie asked her mother, "Is Grandma going to be okay?"

Her mother, Mary, told her what a fighter Grandma was. Later that night Mattie's Grandma died. It was only two days after she saw her Grandma's spirit in the woods walking to Mary's house with the fishing pole.

Mattie's world totally changed that fateful night.

～๑☆๑ ๑๑ ๑☆๑ ๑๑ ๑☆๑ ๑

Mattie's precognitions also included events that happened in my life. Some were funny. Other times, well not so much.

In my pre-teen years, I resisted Mattie's suggestions. I knew she had special gifts, but I was opposed to acknowledging any of it at that stage of my life.

At 13, I was rushing to get out the door on my way to school one morning. I paused to hear the weather report on television before leaving. The local weatherman predicated a clear, warm, sunny day. Yeah, I thought what a great forecast. I loved walking with my friends back and forth to school a couple of miles away. I grabbed my book bag and started out the door.

Mattie called me back, "Don't forget your umbrella."

"What?" the weatherman just said clear, sunny and warm today.

"You better take your umbrella," Mattie insisted.

"Mom, no! I'm gonna look stupid carrying that umbrella! My friends will think I'm crazy!" I pleaded. Teenage girls always want to look cool.

Mattie relented and just said, "Okay."

The junior high school I attended was a new architectural design. Modular with no windows, as a result, I could not stay abreast of the weather conditions outside. Why should I care anyway? The weatherman on television said clear, sunny and warm. It was the final period of the day and we were about to break between classes when I heard a loud BOOM!

I looked at my classmate and asked her, "What was that?"

She said, "It sounds like thunder."

"It can't be," I said. Oh no! Mom cannot be right again, I thought.

The bell rang and school let out for the day. I slowly retrieved my book bag from my locker. If I had my umbrella, I would look like the smartest girl at school. I should have listened to Mom, I thought shaking my head. I'll be soaking wet by time I get home and I deserve it. Why didn't I listen to her?

When I got to the front door at school the downpour was massive. I took a deep breath and started walking swiftly. I got two blocks away from school when I heard the honk of a car horn. I looked up to see Mattie in our station wagon. I hastily crossed the street to get in the car.

"Thank you, mommy," I said.

"You're welcome," she replied. Once inside the car, no other words were spoken on that drive home.

That was a turning point for me. If Mattie told me something, I listened.

~☆~ ~☆~ ~☆~

Sometimes things are just unexplainable. One mysterious event in 1967 actually saved our lives. We lived in a large, old house in the inner city of Kansas City. One day when the lights started flickering unexpectedly, at first, Mattie thought it was just the light bulb going out in the lamp, so she did nothing. A few minutes later while walking to another room she flipped the switch for the ceiling light. It flickered a couple seconds and then the bulb burned out. The third warning came when the TV cut itself off. Mattie went downstairs to check the fuse box in the basement. Everything seemed okay so we went to bed.

Mattie always kept a flashlight in her bedroom tucked in the top drawer of her dresser. In the early morning, the flashlight came on. She was startled at a light she saw peeking through the cracks of the drawers. "How did that happen?" she wondered aloud. She got up, went over to the wooden Chester drawer and turn off the flashlight. Still a little confused, Mattie got back in bed and pulled the covers up. Just as she was about to roll over to go back to sleep she heard a clicking noise. She looked over to find the flashlight had come on again.

Mattie sat straight up and stared at the drawer that seems to be glowing even more than before. She had a foreboding feeling. "What are you trying to tell me?" she asked aloud. In a rush of recent memories, she thought about the flickering lights from the day before. Grabbing the flashlight, she went down to the basement. Moving swiftly from side to side, Mattie let the beam from the flashlight guide her. The beam first hit along the basement walls then the ceiling. Finally, the light illuminated a wire and Mattie saw sparks flying.

Mattie ran upstairs, screaming my name. "D'Nita! Get up, get up!" She dialed zero on the phone, "I need the police!" she said anxiously.

I scrambled trying to get my shoes on before running toward the door. It was dark outside, the wee hours of the morning. The police arrived and Mattie explained the situation. The police officers contacted the gas company. Our neighbors across the street let us sit in their living room while gas company technicians worked on the problem.

The police officers and gas company technicians came to tell us how lucky we were. "Lady, if you waited another 30 minutes, this house would have blown up. Your aging wires were frayed. The sparks you saw in the basement from the wiring was just about to ignite the gas line."

Mattie always said that flickering flashlight was a kind of special magic. That flashlight triggered her memory of the odd electrical occurrences that happen that day. It was her warning that she noticed the problem and got help from the gas company before the house exploded. Sometimes the magic isn't always about what happens. Sometimes the magic is about a disaster averted.

✦

There are many types of hauntings. The scariest Mattie and I experienced was intelligent or interactive haunting activity. For us, this meant an angry spirit who had unfinished business.

We still lived in the big, old house in the inner city. The old house in Vineyard Woods was rented out to Mr. and Mrs. Jones and their two kids. The family seemed nice and everything ran smoothly—for six months.

Around the seventh month Mattie discovered that more people were living in our Vineyard Woods home. As it turned out, the Jones family included nine kids. Seven of those *kids* were actually adults. It appeared all nine kids and some grandkids were living there at various times.

Mattie was livid. When they stopped paying rent, she sent several letters and even threatened legal action if something wasn't done. When Mr. Jones finally contacted Mattie he was hostile and belligerent with her on the phone. Like Dr. Jekyll and Mr. Hyde, this formerly nice man who rented the house became evil. Mattie didn't know he had been an alcoholic for years. Mr. Jones' wife and kids feared him and so did the Vineyard Woods neighbors. He used his large size to intimidate his adult children. He forced them to make threatening calls to us, insisting he would harm Mattie and me.

Eventually Mattie filed papers with the proper court to have the family removed from the house. Mrs. Jones called Mattie. She pleaded with her. "Please don't put the family out," she said. Mrs. Jones told Mattie that Mr. Jones was terminally ill with psoriasis of the liver. In the background Mattie could hear Mr. Jones cursing her for trying to put the family out. Mattie gave the family 60 days to find a new place to live.

A couple weeks before the eviction, Mr. Jones died. The family thought his death would give them more time, but Mattie was firm. The family hadn't paid their rent in seven months. Mattie asked them to leave the house on their own to avoid being physically removed from the premises by the police.

The whole family packed up and left. Well, not quite everyone.

Mattie had folded her daycare and no longer needed that larger inner-city home. She put it up for sale and decided that we would move back into the Vineyard Woods home. I was ecstatic. The Vineyard Woods house needed a complete remodeling. After four months of rehabbing we were back home. We had no idea what awaited us.

In the beginning I was unaware of the hauntings. Mattie shielded me from them. She experienced strange moments where I was unsure of what was happening. One night after I went to bed, Mattie opened my door waking me, asking if I was okay. When my eyes focused, and with the help of the hall light, I saw Mattie was completely naked. I thought, Mom are you alright? I asked her what was wrong. She said she heard a weird sound coming from my room.

Reality set in one afternoon when Mattie left me sleeping, while she went to the Laundromat. I awoke to wailing, moaning and screaming sounds. I thought it might be Mattie crying, so I called out for her. No response. I was terrified and called my dad. He told me to call the police; so I did.

The police dispatcher told me they didn't have enough officers to come every time someone heard strange sounds. The dispatcher asked me how old I was. I told him 13. He told me at age 13 I was too old to be afraid of sounds in the house. So I hung on, but I noticed the time I was speaking to the dispatch I didn't hear those strange sounds. Every time I got on the phone the sounds stopped. It was as if the spirit was watching my moves.

As soon as I hung up the phone the moaning started up again. My last resort was to call my neighbor. She was like a second mother to me. She said she would come as soon as she got someone to watch her kids.

I remember her saying to me, "You know, you're going to have to come out of your room to unlock the door. I don't have a key."

"I will as soon as you get to the porch," I said, voice shaking. It seemed like it took forever for her to reach me. I tried covering my ears, but still the moaning continued.

Finally, she arrived. I bolted for the door as fast as I could, opened the door, and ran out. She came in and walked around. Of course, she did not see or hear anything. Thankfully she took me back to her house until Mattie returned from the Laundromat.

The neighbor called our house every so often to see if Mattie was back. Finally, Mattie answered saying she was just walking in the house with one of the laundry baskets. Our neighbor told her I was at her house. She explained I heard moaning sounds in the house. Mattie drove around the corner to get me. On the way back home Mattie apologized. She told me strange things had been happening in the house since moving in, but she didn't tell me about it since they hadn't bothered me yet.

"I promise not to leave you alone in the house ever again," she said.

After that, sometimes lights would flicker, doors would close, the floors would squeak. Our Chihuahua, Thunder, would hide under the bed. There was an instance when footprints actually appeared as the Spirit walked over newspaper on the floor.

One morning Mattie awoke to a vibrating bed around dawn. Thinking it might be an earthquake, Mattie grabbed the sides of the bed for security. When the tremors stopped, she slowly sat up on the side of the bed. Glancing around her room she noticed nothing was disturbed. Everything was in its rightful place. At that moment she felt something touch her leg. She jerked away and walked swiftly to her bedroom door, then down the hall to my bedroom.

Slowly, she opened my door asking, "Baby, are you okay?"

"Yes momma, why?" I asked.

"Did you feel a tremor like an earthquake?" She probed.

"No, I didn't feel anything momma."

"Okay, go back to sleep," she replied.

Mattie closed my door and I rolled over attempting to sleep again. I pulled the bedcovers over my head as a chill suddenly came over my body. I tossed and turned for a while before calling her back to my room.

"I think I'm getting sick. I have chills," I told her

Mattie felt my forehead, "You are warm," she said. "I need to take your temperature".

"Yeah, you're running a slight fever." Walking back to the medicine cabinet she told me she would give me an aspirin, hoping it would help.

I took two aspirin and once again, I pulled the covers over my head. To no avail, I just could not get warm. The room seemed like it was freezing cold. "Mom, this room is freezing," I shouted.

She walked in. "The room really is freezing," she said. Checking all the vents, Mattie looked very concerned. Retrieving a few blankets from the hall closet, she told me to lie down on the living room sofa. I tried watching television, but the screen showed static off and on. I drifted off to sleep.

I awoke to Mattie banging the kitchen cabinet doors. Groggy with sleep, I tried to focus on what she was doing. She was moving very fast, going from one side of the kitchen to the other. She kept aimlessly looking inside the kitchen cabinets, opening and closing the doors.

"Mom, what's going on?" I asked

Speaking quickly she said, "Soup. I'm trying to find soup. I got to get some soup."

I just put the pillow over my head again and tried to get back to sleep. I finally fell asleep when Mattie woke me up again informing me she had to go to the grocery store to buy food, including soup. She insisted I go to the store with her. Mattie explained I could take my blanket and lay down in the back seat of the car.

"Mom I don't' want to go," I whined.

"You can't stay here," she insisted. Her voice was still was on high speed. "I'll have to get someone to stay with you."

"No mom, I just want to sleep." I was angry, at a point of exhaustion and dared the "boogey man" to bother me.

Mattie stared at me.

I turned over on the sofa in frustration. "I want to sleep, mom."

Mattie put on her coat and grabbed her car keys.

Drifting off to sleep I faintly heard Mattie pull up the garage door. She started the car. A few seconds later I was rattled awake by a loud roar followed quickly by a big boom. I jumped up to look out the window. I fell to my knees screaming, I couldn't believe what I saw.

Mattie's car plowed off a section of the garage across the street. The car was moving backwards, up the hill. Then the car rammed backwards into another house. The car finally stopped, thanks to a fence pole lodged in its grille.

I ran out of the house toward the car screaming, "Mommy, mommy!" I could not see her inside the car. As I got closer, her head suddenly popped up and she got out of the car.

"Mommy, I couldn't see you I thought you were dead!"

"Mattie said, "I was trying to find my wig. It fell on the floorboard."

"What happened?" I asked, still shaking.

Mattie explained when she put the car in reverse, the gas pedal stuck to the floor. She stepped on the brake, but it did not stop the car no matter how hard she pressed. All she could think to do was steer the car to avoid driving directly through the house across the street. She knew small children lived there. Mattie thanked her lucky stars for the magic that prevented her "possessed" car from harming the children that were standing in the front window looking out at the street when her car slammed into a corner of the house. According to Mattie magic was also at play when the car finally ended up with a fence pole slammed into the grille where it couldn't hurt anyone.

Our neighbors had already called the police. Arriving with the police were a couple local television news crews. Mattie yelled at them not to put her on camera as she walked back to our house with one of the police officers.

※

Mattie announced we were leaving the Vineyard Woods house. She said, "What happened to this car is no coincidence. Something has been building all day long."

We left the next day with one of Mattie's friends to get a horseshoe to nail over the front door. Folklore says if you nail a horseshoe over the door with the ends pointed up, it will repel evil spirits. We were willing to try anything.

Mattie and I stayed closed to each other even sleeping together until moving day two months later. Thankfully Mr. Jones did not follow us to the next house.

★　　　★　　　★

Life Lessons

I realize this chapter is controversial to some people with certain religious beliefs. People of different faiths hold different ideas about what happens to the spirit immediately after our physical death. My mother and I respect people with different opinions. We have never tried to persuade anyone to believe our point of view. I am simply writing about the events that touched our lives. It has moved me closer to my understanding of the Divine Creator and the Universe.

Keep an open mind: I encourage you to remain skeptical. However, I just hope you can keep an open mind and entertain the idea that anything is possible.

If you can stay open to the possibilities, ask yourself these questions:

- ☐ Have you ever experienced déjà vu moments? Even if that experience simply started as a dream?

- ☐ Have you ever had strong feelings that something is going to happen to you or to someone else?

- ☐ Are you able to actually feel others' emotions?

☐ Do you get visions or mental images of some events?

☐ Do you occasionally think about someone and then, that person calls you, or, you see them shortly afterward?

☐ Do you ever catch a glimpse of something out of the corner of your eye?

If you can honestly answer "yes" to any of these questions, do not ignore these signs. They are real supernatural powers. You can proudly say you possess specials gifts. You are closely connected to your mind and body. Be proud of the fact that you have supernatural powers.

Make use of Your Unusual Gift: The highest and best use of your gift is to help others. Understand that each person possesses unique gifts from the Divine Creator or God. These gifts vary. *Aerona* is a person who has the ability to see and understand all forms of illness, whether it is physical or mental. There have been reports of the gift of *Weather Control*. It is a power that allows a person to actually influence weather patterns. Whatever gifts you possess were given to you by the Creator. Therefore, the Creator should be the inspiration behind all spiritual gifts. Consider how blessed you are to experience the beauty of God's many spiritual gifts.

☆   ☆   ☆

FORGIVE THOSE THAT TRESPASS

"The weak can never forgive. Forgiveness is the attribute of the strong." — Mahatma Gandhi

"I've made some huge mistakes." John spoke from his heart. He continued, "Mattie please forgive me for everything I've put you though. I'm so sorry for all the pain I caused you."

"It's okay." Mattie reassured him.

Flashback

Almost two years after my brother Robert's death, my mom Mattie started letting me see my father John again. Her decision was met with serious opposition from our family and friends. Then there were the gossipmongers at the beauty salon. The gossipmongers spread their own version of the events leading up to my brother's death. They eventually forced Mattie to only work with a select clientele in her business.

My relationship with John was odd. He genuinely tried to do father-like things with me. For instance, he bought me my first "big-girl" bicycle. I loved that bike. I remember riding up and down the street, while he sat proudly in his favorite chair on the porch watching me. He would buy me toys and games I wanted for my bedroom at his house. Then, he would stand in the doorway watching me play alone. He didn't know how to sit on the floor and play with me. But he did seem to love watching over me.

There were many awkward moments with my father. Anytime there was a need for a real in-depth, father-daughter conversation, we were usually silent instead.

I didn't understand my father or how he went about things. He never mentioned my mother in a negative manner. However, he would tell me what a pathetic family I came from. Strangely enough, he thought it wouldn't bother me to hear these things; it did.

By the time I turned 12, I was at my wits end. I was so fed up with the variety of his bad-mouthing my family; I refused to visit him for a while. I made up excuses. Finally, he figured out that I was purposely avoiding him.

A couple months later he called Mattie, crying over the phone, wanting to know why I refused to see him. She explained to him I was tired of his constantly bashing her side of the family. It upset me. He asked to speak to me and apologized over the phone. He promised he would not do it again. He kept his word for a while, but it was short-lived. Soon I became upset with him for bad-mouthing my family all over again.

Mattie encouraged me to visit my father, citing her strained relationship with her own father as an example of what she did not want for me. "Your father loves you, baby. I know he has a strange way of showing you." She said, "I wish my father wanted to spend time with me when I was your age like your father does. Maybe my life would've turned out differently."

As an adult, I was amazed Mattie never used me as a pawn or a weapon against John. It was simply how Mattie handled things. Even if she was frustrated with him, she never talked badly about him to me. She had incredible strength and discretion.

John never spoke to me about my brother, Robert. He never brought up what happen that fateful day, not one single time. It was clear that the guilt of it haunted him. For example, one day I was sitting in a chair in the living room when he walked in. He screamed at me to get up. I was so scared, immediately I jumped up and ran to the other side of the room. He had never raised his voice like that to me before. Once safely on the other side of the room, I stared at him as he stared at the chair I just leapt away from.

He said, "I don't want you sitting by that gun."

I thought what he is talking about? Then I noticed his hunting gun in its case lying against the wall. It was right behind where I was sitting.

I did not know what to say, I just replied, "Okay I won't."

I couldn't wait to tell mom what happened. She was not surprised.

She said, "I can imagine your father lives with a lot of guilt. He's still living in the very same house where everything happened." She actually seemed empathic.

Mattie insisted that John co-parent. I am sure her desire to have a father present in my life stemmed from the void left by her own absent father.

A couple of totally different events stand out. Both events shaped my character, as I matured. My parents actually worked together to surprise me at my Baptism.

John hated church. Mattie and I attended regularly. He hated the minister, maybe even more than the church. So, one day I gently told him I was being baptized in church by the minister.

"Dad I just want you to know I'm getting baptized on June 14th at 6:00 pm at the church."

"Okay," he replied simply.

I'm not sure what I was expecting but a big part of me wanted him to say he would attend. Another part of me was just glad he didn't yell or lecture me about how much he hated church again.

On June 14th, I was baptized along with my best friend. Afterward, my fellow re-born Christians and I stood at the front of the church to be greeted by well-wishers. To my great surprise John was first in line with a huge grin on his face. He gave me a big bear hug and a kiss on my cheek. I couldn't believe it.

Mattie was standing in the front row with a smile. She knew he would be there all along.

～♪☆ℓ～ℐℂ～♪☆ℓ～ℐℂ～♪☆ℓ～ℐ

Fast Forward to Christmas 1973

I knew John was not feeling well. Christmas was fast approaching and I wanted to do something special for him. I had matured into a 16-year-old at the time. Mattie laughed and said, "How about surprising him with a live Christmas tree?" She laughed because John still put up the old, aluminum tree with the revolving spotlight from the 1960s. Mattie and I shared a *knowing* laugh together. She said, "Let's make the tree a surprise." I called him when we got home to tell him I would be over the next weekend to help him put up the old aluminum tree.

102

Mattie and I got up early one Saturday morning in December to go Christmas tree shopping. We just wanted a small tree. Something we could handle ourselves. We went to Jimmy's Christmas Trees in Kansas City and were greeted by an elf. We told the elf we wanted a five to six-foot-tall tree, and he promptly took us to that section of the tree lot. I saw the perfect Christmas tree and screamed, "That's the one! Let's get that one!" A bigger elf secured a string around the tree and collected the money and wished us a Merry Christmas.

Mattie piped up, "Oh yeah, we need a tree stand, too."

The big elf leaned the tree up against the makeshift house to get a tree stand for us. Then, Mattie and I carried the tree back to the car and wrestled it into the station wagon.

On the trip to his house Mattie said, "I'm glad we're doing this for your dad. I don't think he's as well as he pretends."

"Do you think Dad's real sick?" I asked.

"I just think he's not feeling as well as he wants us to think." she reassured me.

When we finally arrived at his house I told Mattie I wanted to drag the tree up to the front door by myself. Mattie offered to help me carry it. "That tree's too heavy for you," she said. We struggled with the tree and finally got it to the door. Mattie rang the doorbell, and then she walked back to the car. I posed with the tree impatiently waiting in silence for John to open the door. He finally opened the door. His eyes grew wide like a little boy opening the big present on Christmas morning. He let out a hearty laugh. "Tired of the old tree I guess," he said still laughing. He gave me a hug and waved to Mattie who was standing by the car. As I watched Mattie in the driveway, standing there smiling, it felt as though we were almost a normal family again.

Mattie was right, John wasn't as well as he pretended. He developed diabetes a year earlier. He casually told Mattie he had the disease. Quickly he added, "Don't tell the baby. I'm okay," he insisted.

His relationship with people in his neighborhood was usually combative. The neighborhood was multi-ethnic, yet no one was immune to his rants. Anyone who stepped a foot on his property, without his permission, he threatened to shoot. After my brother's death, his reputation put fear in some of the neighbors. He unwisely inflated his already dangerous reputation with his shouts and threats to shoot anyone who came on his property without permission. There were a couple neighbors he didn't scare off. Over the years he developed a friendly rapport with them. Later in life those relationships proved invaluable. Thankfully, those people saw past his angry, blustering exterior to his heart deep inside. Often, he buried his heart so deep even he forgot he had one.

Over the next few months Mattie and I noticed changes in John. He stopped driving himself to the store and to his medical appointments. Those kind neighbors took his grocery order and actually delivered his food to him. Mattie started fixing monstrous amounts of food on Sundays. We would take it over to him and he would eat it throughout the week.

He was old-fashioned and hated the idea of fast food, even though he never tried it. One day, after school, Mattie and I dropped over at his house to check on him. Mattie asked him if wanted anything because we were stopping by McDonalds.

"No fast food. I hate it," he said.

When we arrived at MacDonald's Mattie paid for my order and got an extra Big Mac for him.

"Mom, Dad isn't going to eat that," I said.

"We'll see," she replied with a wry grin, looking like she would take that bet.

When we arrived, John opened the door looking at the MacDonald sack and said, "Mmm-mm, that does smell good," as we walked past. Mattie and I sat at the huge dining room table side-by-side, opened our meals and started eating our burgers and fries.

John sat down.

After watching us take a couple bites, he asked, "Can I taste that?'

Mattie told him we bought a Big Mac just for him.

John had that, "Oh-you-shouldn't-have" look on his face, but gladly took his Big Mac. We watched closely as he took his first bite of fast food. After his third or fourth bite, Mattie asked him how it tasted.

He said, "This is good, I like this."

Mattie and I laughed.

John, a diehard against anything progressive was actually eating fast food and loving it. The next week he asked us if we would bring him that hamburger again when we came by.

As the months passed he became increasingly weaker. We had no idea he was no longer taking his diabetes medicine. The doctor he trusted had passed away and he was no longer able to refill his prescriptions. Unfortunately, he refused to go see another doctor. His fear was the next prescription to treat his diabetes might be insulin injections.

July 3, 1974

John had an incredibly difficult week. Mattie and I were at his house every day making sure he ate. He gave us a key to the house because he did not even want to come downstairs from his bedroom.

"Going to the hospital is not an option," he said.

That evening we left around 7:00 pm, a little earlier than usual because I was not feeling well. John lay down and said he would be fine, but we promised to call as soon as we got home anyway just to make sure.

When we arrived home we called as promised. There was no answer. Mattie said, "Let's give him ten minutes. He might be in the bathroom." I called back again in ten minutes and there was still no answer.

"We need to go back over there," Mattie insisted as she tried a third time unsuccessfully to reach him. We quickly threw a few things in overnight bags stopping only to make one last attempt to reach him on the phone. Mattie and I rushed to the car and drove back to his house, afraid of what we might find.

Opening the door to John's house, Mattie and I called his name. We were relieved when we heard him shout back from upstairs. He said he was using the bathroom and was too weak to get up. Mattie and I started climbing the stairs when he asked that only Mattie come up to help him from the bathroom back to bed. I heard both of them struggle. He was six foot two and despite his illness he still weighed 200 pounds. Once back in bed I was allowed upstairs.

John's pride and dignity was still intact, I remember thinking.

Mattie and I tried everything we could think of to talk him into going to the hospital that evening.

He relented a bit, saying, "If I'm not better by morning you can take me to the hospital."

"Do you promise Dad?" I asked.

"Yes baby, I promise."

I made my way downstairs. As I reached the bottom of the stairs I noticed a large white book on a stand at the end of the buffet table. I had never noticed it before. I crossed the room to get a better look and couldn't believe it. It was a beautiful oversized white leather Bible. John was actually reading the Bible.

Mattie joined me downstairs and I showed her the Bible. Mattie said she was happy he was finding peace.

I asked Mattie where we would sleep for the night knowing we would have to stay with him. She said, "There's a sofa bed in the living room. It'll be interesting to see what condition it's in." As we yanked it open, years of dust flew out. Mattie and I cleaned and cleaned. We were happy to find clean sheets that fit the sofa bed. We slipped between the covers and shouted "Goodnight!" to John upstairs.

Just as we got cozy we heard a loud boom of thunder, then the sound of hail hitting the windows. I put the pillow over my head and we both drifted off to sleep. Minutes later we heard a different boom coming from upstairs. We both popped out of bed and started for the stairs. Mattie stopped me and told me to wait, "If I need you, I'll call you." Waiting at the bottom of the stairs, I heard my parent's voices and the sound of a struggle. I waited a few minutes then quietly I crept up the stairs.

Standing outside my father's room I saw my parents sitting side-by-side on his bed. John told Mattie he had some financial things he needed to change. He called his sisters on the phone and asked them to come out from Texas to Kansas City. They replied the earliest they could arrive was on Friday evening as it was almost Thursday. After he hung up the phone, Mattie remained silent and let him speak.

"I've made some huge mistakes," he said. He gently laid his head on Mattie's shoulder. He tilted his head back so he could look directly in her eyes.

"Mattie, please forgive me for everything I put you though. I'm so sorry for the pain I caused you."

"It's okay." Mattie reassured him.

"I can't believe you're here helping me. I'm the person who hurt you the most. Would you please forgive me?" he asked Mattie

"I forgave you years ago, John." She responded

Mattie noticed me standing in the hall.

I spoke up, "Is everything okay? What happened?"

Mattie explained he had fallen out of bed but was okay. She lifted his legs helping him lay back down. I walked over to him and asked, "You sure you're okay, Dad?"

"Yes," he said in a weak voice.

I went back downstairs to get in the sofa bed and Mattie followed. In bed we talked face-to-face, though we could barely see each other in the darkness. I asked her if it felt strange sleeping in this house again. She answered, "Yes, a little," We both sighed about the same time. I thought about how bizarre the evening was and drifted to sleep again.

We were awakened by yet another boom from upstairs

"Mom, you think that was Dad again?" I asked

"Yes, I'll go up and check. You stay down here this time," she instructed.

I was too tired to argue and stayed in bed. Nodding off I heard Mattie call me from upstairs.

"Baby can you come up here, I need help."

I jumped out of bed and ran upstairs. He had fallen out of bed again. This time Mattie couldn't get him back in bed herself.

She said, "Grab his feet and help me lift."

Together we put Dad back in bed. Then she instructed me to stand by the door. We were face-to-face as she looked me in the eye and said, "I believe John has passed. I'm going to call the operator and get an ambulance."

I let loud a loud scream.

She told me to be strong and wait on the ambulance.

Then she said, "I'm not a doctor, I could be wrong. Maybe he's in a diabetic coma."

The look in her eyes told me she had seen enough death to know the truth.

I ran downstairs, sat on the side of the sofa bed and cried. Mattie called the operator and explained the situation. An ambulance arrived within minutes. The crew went upstairs to check on John. Mattie found his address book and was on the phone explaining to his sisters what was happening.

A few minutes later the nurse came downstairs to tell us he had passed.

I cried and the nurse held me. She told me as next of kin I had to sign and date the papers to let them take his body away. I was still sixteen, just days away from my next birthday. So, I signed and dated the papers July 4th, 1973.

The nurse told me to turn my back to the foyer because they were bringing his body down the stairs. As I turned to face the fireplace, I let my eyes glance around the room at all the 'things' it contained. My mind raced and I thought; all the things my parents fought about and fought over during their divorce were so unimportant now. I sat on the floor and cried as I heard the sounds of paramedics bringing his body down the stairs and take him out the front door. As the screen door closed behind the paramedics, Mattie reached down to help me get up from the floor and held me. I kept repeating over and over, "He promised he would go to the hospital this morning. Why couldn't he wait?"

Mattie told me to always remember how much he loved me. She said, "I don't think it was a coincidence we were all under the same roof tonight. It's the magic. No way any of us would have believed this was possible after your brother's death. Your father's at peace now."

I told her I overheard their conversation about forgiveness. She said, "Yes I forgave your dad years ago so I could live."

★   ★   ★

Life Lessons

I was not yet open to forgiveness. Forgiving myself, that is. I sometimes thought I was the one who instigated the perpetual problems between my parents. I felt everything was fine until my birth. My mom was there to reassure me it wasn't my fault.

My Aunts, John's sisters, hinted Mattie and I had to be responsible for John's death. According to them, it was impossible for Mattie to be such a compassionate human being when you consider the pain he "supposedly" put her through: the nasty divorce and the death of my brother, Robert. So, in their eyes, we must have done something to hasten his death. My aunts' theory was it was some kind of payback for Robert's death.

My father was born in Waller County, Texas and his family had their burial tombs plots there. So his funeral and burial were there. I wanted my father's wake in Kansas City. I wanted those who helped him in his final days to have a chance to say goodbye. His sisters were the Executors of the Will and in charge of his insurance policies. They fought me on the wake. In their minds everything should be held in Texas. I was furious! In the end I won having my father's wake in Kansas City. The two funeral homes worked together to make the transition smooth from Kansas City to Texas.

Mom and I had just settled on the visiting hours at the funeral home when another bombshell hit. Anita, mother's "friend" who ended up having an affair with my father many years ago, left a message with the funeral home asking if she could attend the visitation.

I shouted, "No!" I was so incensed in the moment. I was not ready to forgive.

A few days later, while cleaning things out in his house, I found letters his sisters wrote him. The letters said, "There is no way the girl is your child." They never even used my name, D'Nita or Dee. They just called me "the girl" in all the letters. I was fuming mad! I thought there was no way I could forgive them. They contribute to my parents' problems.

Mattie tried to be a calming voice of reason. After the drama surrounding my father's death and burial had subsided, I sat in my bedroom and did a lot of thinking. I remembered vividly my parent's emotional conversation as he was finally nearing death and him asking Mattie for forgiveness. Mattie had forgiven him years earlier. Her ability to do what was right and not hold a grudge or seek revenge was incredible. So many family members and friends alike tried to tell her what to do over the years. I knew I had to find a way to move on as well.

I asked Mattie how she could move forward and forgive so easily. She explained to me at the time of their divorce and later after Robert's sudden death, her reaction to her hurt and pain was to feel she would never forgive him. Later she began asking herself a few important questions that changed her mind.

Who Suffers? Often when she thought about that Saturday afternoon when Robert died, her pain was rekindled. Once reminded, she started thinking how bad it was. How unfair. After all, my brother did not deserve to die. Mattie said she would feel the anger and resentment building inside her. Then she would feel the depths of her despair. She would silently say repeatedly, "I'll never forgive him."

At this point, she figured who was feeling bad. Who was miserable? The answer? She was the one hurting most.

The resentment and bitterness was crippling to her body and was detrimental to her health and her ability to enjoy her life. She had to let it go. Mattie said she had to clear the anger from her heart so she could live. She said forgiveness was freeing.

Why is it so Difficult? If forgiveness is freeing why did I find it difficult just to forgive my Aunts and Anita? After all, what they did was inexcusable. Mattie said maybe I associated forgiveness with somehow being weak or giving in. Mattie continued, "Maybe, you worry forgiving might be an invitation to be mistreated again. Also, not forgiving can give us sense of power and control by holding onto a grudge." Mattie told me she went through all that, "This is not the path you want to go, baby."

Forgiveness empowers you. It puts you back in charge of you. Mattie reminded me forgiveness gives us a choice. The choice is, "Do you want to be bitter or feel better. Keep holding onto the pain and you'll be bitter. Make the better choice. Learn to let go. Learn to be a forgiving person."

It didn't happen overnight but eventually, gradually I learned to follow Mattie's example and become a forgiving person.

★   ★   ★

FATHER HUNGER

"The father wound is epidemic among us."—Gordon Dalbey

When Mattie finally passed at 78, she had married five times. I believe the major reason for her multiple marriages had to do with searching for the affection she never received from either her father or her stepfather. Although she always tried to show her strong side, inside was a little girl starving for attention and love from a man.

Mattie felt different from most people in the African-American community. When she was born there were whispers and gossip that perhaps she was the landowner owner's child. She looked different: her nose hooked, she had freckles and reddish-brown curly hair. As she grew, Mattie thought differently from others, too. She was always wondering, hoping, and wishing for something a little better. She always knew there was something better out there for her; however, she did not always know the best way to get there.

Mattie left her home and her family at the tender age of twelve after blowing up at Mr. Douce the landowner. She spent the next three years doing odd jobs, living wherever and with whomever she could, one night to the next. Even though her clothes and shoes were well-worn, she tried desperately to hold her head high. Some young women in the community turned their noses up at her. Others openly teased and mocked her.

As a young teen, Mattie caught the eye of a young man a few years older than she. He was well-liked with the popular crowd, especially with the ladies. Mattie felt uncomfortable when he started turning his affections toward her.

He tried talking with her and asked her, "What's your name?"

Mattie, looking down at her feet, was slow to answer him. "Mattie Pearl," she replied softly.

He broadly said, "My name's Robert. I'm glad to meet you."

"Where do you live Mattie Pearl?" he asked her.

Mattie shrugged her shoulders and refused to answer. She looked around and saw a couple neighborhood girls whispering behind her back. As the other girls started walking closer, Mattie turned to walk away from them. After a few steps she looked back. Those girls had a firm grip on his arms as if to say he belongs with us, not you. At least she felt that way.

Each day Robert crossed paths with Mattie Pearl to try and talk with her. She resisted telling him much about herself. Gradually she grew more comfortable with him. Soon a friendship developed. She was still uncomfortable with the romantic relationships he maintained with several ladies.

When Mattie lost a steady job as housekeeper, she also lost a place to live. She snuck food from the nearby farm fields in the evening. At night, she took refuge and slept in a nearby barn. Ashamed and embarrassed, she told no one where she was sleeping at night.

While looking for work, she noticed Robert, but tried to avoid him. He spotted her and began walking toward her. He drilled her about her whereabouts. She gave only evasive answers and he pretended not to care. But one day he followed her, staying far enough behind so she would not hear his footsteps. She walked through the fields with him not far behind. Mattie stopped to pick peaches and plums. Robert watched as she entered the barn with a few pieces of fruit. He waited for her to come out. When she didn't, he realized this was where she was staying. He never let on that he knew about it.

Robert knew Mattie usually came into town every three to four days. One day he was sure she would be there. Everyone knew this was the day food samples from the best cooks were provided for free. Robert spotted her and casually walked over to talk.

"Mattie, I have something I want to tell you."

Curious she asked him, "What?"

"You're going to marry me!" he exclaimed, smiling broadly.

"I am?" Mattie was puzzled.

"Yes you. And, it'll be in the next couple days." Robert said confidently.

Mattie was speechless.

Finally, she asked, "Why do you want to marry me and not one of those other pretty girls?"

Robert said, "I like you better. Okay?"

He told Mattie to get her things. She would stay with his family.

She told him she really didn't have 'things' to get.

He said, "I'll fix that."

Feeling unloved and abandoned, Mattie Pearl was quick to accept his proposal. After all she captured the heart of a handsome, older man. Suddenly she was envied by the other young, attractive women in the community.

Robert and Mattie were married at his family's house. Quickly, she settled into the routine of married life. Within a few weeks after their wedding day she was pregnant. Nine months after that, she gave birth to Robert Jr., my brother, after less than a year of marriage.

As a husband and father, Robert Sr. was a domineering man. He treated his young bride as his underling. With all the responsibilities of a new infant, she did not get out of the house much, but when she did, she was greeted with gossip that her husband was still romantically involved with his former girlfriend. Mattie tolerated the gossip. It was all hearsay. She wanted to believe he wouldn't do that to her and their young family.

It all came to a head one day when Mattie caught Robert Sr. red-handed with one of his former girlfriends. He didn't seem to mind getting caught. It also didn't bother him when Mattie said she wanted out of the marriage. If she wanted out, it would only come with stipulations. The biggest one was that she must leave her son Robert Jr. until she found suitable work.

C~9☆C~9C~9☆C~9C~9☆C~9

In the early 1940s Mattie was a new resident of Kansas City. She made good money working in an ammunition plant during WWII. On the weekends, she enjoyed watching the Negro League baseball team, the Kansas City Monarchs. On the top of her list were the Kansas City jazz clubs. She loved listening to music and dancing the night away in the historic

12th-18th and Vine district. It was there she met both her best friend for life, and her second husband.

Mattie became friendly with the regulars at the clubs located on 18th and Vine. She formed a bond with one woman in particular, Leatha. Mattie was a more gregarious than Leatha. So, Mattie was always pushing Leatha to try new things, the latest restaurant or new dance moves.

One Friday evening Mattie and Leatha met a couple brothers. In the distance the brothers looked white but as they approach the ladies they looked like they could possibly be Negroes. The brothers were tall, slender, and handsome. They asked Mattie and Leatha to join them at their table for cocktails. Mattie quickly agreed. But Leatha hesitated. After some serious nudging, by Mattie and the brothers, Leatha finally agreed.

The first brother held out his arm for Mattie. She held on tightly as they strolled across the room to the brothers' table. As her escort politely pulled out a chair for her, she looked back to see Leatha walking nervously towards their table. After Leatha was seated, the questions started. Mattie was first to ask.

"I see your brothers. What are your names?"

Mattie's escort replied his name was John and the other brother said his name was Willie.

Mattie spoke again, "John and Willie do you have last names?" she asked with a twinkle in her eye.

"Littlejohn, John Littlejohn," he replied with a smirk.

Mattie let out a laugh "Really? John Littlejohn?"

"Now don't you laugh at me. That's really my name." Then John let out a hearty laugh.

As the evening drew to a close Leatha gradually warmed up to Willie. They agreed to meet again. Mattie and John agreed to have lunch the next day at John and Willie's Aunt Anna's café.

Leatha whispered to Mattie as they left the club, "I think I've heard of the Littlejohn brothers before."

"What have you heard?" Mattie asked Leatha, laughing.

"They really love the ladies. Did you see how all the other women were looking at them?"

"Well, they were only looking at us tonight," Mattie shot back.

The next afternoon Mattie met up with John for lunch. She enjoyed their conversation. She chatted up her life adventures and told him about her son Robert, Jr. He told Mattie his non-battle war stories from World War II. Mattie discovered John worked in his Uncle's dry-cleaning shop. The more she learned about him the more she liked him. Over the course of the next year John and Mattie grew closer. She spent some days at the home he rented from his cousin. She never stayed with him at night, fearing the negative perception his family might have of her as a result.

One day Leatha told Mattie she had important news to share. So Leatha and Willie joined Mattie at John's house. They were hardly in the door a minute when Leatha blurted out, "Willie asked me to marry him!" Leatha sounded like an excited school girl, even though this would be her second marriage. Mattie's eyes grew wide as she jumped up out of her seat to congratulate and hug Leatha. "I'm so happy for you Leatha!" Mattie joyfully exclaimed. Leatha said she wasn't expecting the proposal. "I'm so happy for the first time in a long time." Leatha thought they would get married at the small church most of the Littlejohn family belonged to. The four of them celebrated at John's house the rest of the evening.

After the celebration, John took Mattie back home. She half expected him to follow suit and ask her to marry him. It seemed like all the brothers tend to operate the same way. Whatever one does, the other follows suit. All Mattie got that night was a goodnight kiss at the door.

Mattie was happy for her friend Leatha, but she felt left out. Bit-by-bit Mattie started picking herself apart. What was she doing wrong? Why wasn't she getting to be part of the Littlejohn family?

When she met up with Leatha again, out of the blue Leatha said, "Wouldn't it be nice if we both got married at the same time?" Mattie let her know John had not proposed to her. Honestly, she was not sure he ever would.

Leatha told Mattie she knew John talked to Willie about it.

"That's why I was so surprised when Willie asked me. I thought John was going to propose to you first," she shared.

"Maybe he changed his mind about me," Mattie said. Her low self-esteem raised its ugly head again.

Leatha did not know what to say, and the silence between them made both young women uncomfortable. Finally, Leatha spoke up, "I'm sure he's waiting for the right moment to ask." They both changed the subject.

From that point forward Mattie tried to play it cool with John. She never mentioned she wanted to hear those words from him. John, however, felt the growing distance between them. She endured another two months of uneasy distance between them before she finally got a proposal of marriage from John. It was not a special occasion. Just a man afraid a good woman might get away if he didn't ask her. At least that's how Mattie explained it to me years later.

It was late on a Sunday afternoon. John and Mattie got dinner from his Aunt's café. As the meal ended, he started acting funny. He was slurring his words, blankly staring into space. Mattie thought he might need medical attention.

"John, are you alright? What's wrong?" she asked.

John words were slowly coming from his mouth. She started getting up from the table thinking she should call someone.

John shouted, "No sit down!"

Instantly Mattie sat back down. The look in her eyes registered surprise.

"I have something to ask you," John said.

Still confused, she sharply replied, "What?"

Finally, he got up and knelt upon one knee, "Will you marry me?" he asked.

Mattie was stunned, "You're asking me to marry you?"

"Yes! Mattie will you marry me?" John repeated as he got up off his knee.

Mattie said, "Oh yes, yes, yes." Then she jumped into his arms.

Six months later, Leatha's dream came true. Both she and Mattie were married in the Littlejohn family church. It was a small, beautiful ceremony with only family in attendance including, her son, Robert Jr. Mattie moved in with John and finally had her ideal house with the white picket fence.

Unfortunately, the illusion of the white picket fence started coming apart quickly, slat by slat. Mattie found out John actually owned nothing. Another member of his family had his name on everything, including his car. Mattie tried to encourage him to start acquiring things they could call their own as a couple. He always agreed with her, but nothing was accomplished.

As months passed, Mattie knew they had totally different ideas of what it meant to be husband and wife. John went to work, came home and sat, relaxing at the end of the day. Mattie went to work, came home and cooked, cleaned, washed and ironed. She discovered the cousin who owned their house kept the exterior of the house and the yard up because as they said, "Cousin John is lazy." Now, all the upkeep on the outside was left to Mattie, too.

One time in an attempt to get his attention, Mattie stopped cooking, cleaning and washing. She gave him an ultimatum. Shape up; stop being lazy or she would be out. Her words fell on deaf ears. He got food from his Aunt's café. He took his dirty clothes to his Uncle's cleaners. Mattie finally realized John and Willie were pampered by their family their entire lives. Their parent died when they were young. So, their extended family picked up the slack and looked after them. After a year and a half Mattie divorced John Littlejohn. Leatha and Willie stayed together as husband and wife until they parted by death many, many years later.

�~ৎ ☆ ℭ~ৎ ℭ~ৎ ☆ ℭ~ৎ ℭ~ৎ ☆ ℭ~ৎ

My parents met in 1949 through a mutual friend. My father John was 15 years older than my mom Mattie. She was intrigued by this older man who held an excellent job. At the time Mattie also had a good job as a salad girl for Macy's in the heart of downtown Kansas City. This younger woman with a big personality, shaped like a curvy Coca-Cola bottle, intrigued him.

In the beginning they were just friends, going out together with other friends. Soon their friendship deepened into love. Mattie got a new job as an Assistant in Fabrics at Macy's. John received a promotion and became a meat inspector for the Amour Meat Packing Company. One evening John

123

unexpectedly asked Mattie, "You want to get married?" A little over a year later, they were married in a civil ceremony. This was Mattie's third marriage and John's first.

A couple years later, he told Mattie they were hiring at Amour. Mattie was trying to get her son Robert Jr., back to Kansas City from Houston. Robert was married now and liked the idea of a good job at Armour. He arranged a job for him and gave his blessing for him, his wife, Audrey, and their new baby daughter to move into the rose-colored house. Robert Jr. and his family were in Kansas City a couple years all living happily under one roof. One day my parents were flabbergasted when Mattie unexpectedly became pregnant. The shock of an unplanned pregnancy and my birth months later sent John into a downward emotional spiral. The chapters on "Run Get Out" and "Dirty Deeds" chronicle his descent.

Mattie's fourth marriage was to Collier. He was discussed in detail in the chapter titled "The Love Bandit". Collier came into Mattie's life when she was the most susceptible and vulnerable to his charms. Her abusive marriage to John, the nasty divorce and the death of Robert Jr. left Mattie exposed. Collier was a predator who used charm, his verbal gifts, and his outgoing personality to manipulate Mattie.

Collier, "the love bandit", befriended and married Mattie in an attempt to get her property, the Vineyard Woods home. He pursued her because she was lonely, hurting, and had a strong desire for intimacy and male support. Mattie's craving for a loving relationship made her willing to go to great extremes and excuse Collier's behavior to satisfy her needs, making her even more vulnerable.

With help from her nephews and her father, Mattie managed to successfully get Collier out of her life. Most of the damage from this failed marriage was to her ego. (Mattie finally formed a bond with her father because of the love bandit.)

In 1967, Mattie married William Brown. It was the fifth and final time she would wed. This marriage was strictly a business deal. Oddly enough, it lasted until death did part them. Mattie and William knew each other for over 20 years before they married. He was a World War II veteran. He saw active battle, and he used alcohol to mask his pain. He was also a chain smoker, another habit he brought from his years in the military. Mattie saw him from time to time, but when he came into her life on a regular basis, he was genuinely trying to improve his life.

He was looking to rent a room. Mattie told him we had a room to spare, but there were certain conditions: First, he could not set foot in the house if he was intoxicated. Second, he could not smoke in the house; period. Third, he had a curfew. If he was not in the house by 1:00 am, he needed to stay wherever he was for the night. Fourth, there would be no entertaining of women in his room. Finally, he had to pay room and board on time. In a way, Mattie was mothering him and taking care of him by laying down these strict rules.

Like a good son he followed the rules dutifully; most of the time. I remember one morning Mattie found his bed, untouched. Concerned, she looked out the window and saw his car outside. She went outside and walked over to his car. As she approached the car, she noticed his feet. She looked in and tapped on the car window to make sure he was okay. He slowly roused back to life. Mattie could tell he had been drinking excessively.

He said, "You told me not to come in the house when I'm drunk."

Mattie replied, "Thank you. If you think you're sober now you can come back in."

William gradually recognized that Mattie was the only person who truly cared about him. It took him a while, but he eventually got his drinking under control.

One day he asked Mattie if he could talk with her about something important.

"Mattie, I want you to marry me." he told a stunned Mattie. "I have benefits coming from the military and a few personal effects. As you know, my family is full of vultures. They only want what they can get from me. After everything I went through in the service, after I'm gone, I want to someone to have those benefits who I know deserves them." Mattie asked him why he was talking about death.

He replied, "You never know what might happen. I want things to be right before anything happens."

Mattie asked, "Are sure you want to do this?"

He replied, "Yes."

They were married in 1967 in a small town in Oklahoma. They chose Oklahoma because they did not want his family knowing anything.

In 1968, William, or "Brownie Boy" as Mattie sometimes called him, fell ill. His cough that we thought was a lingering cold never stopped. He put up a fight until he realized he had no choice but to go see a doctor. Mattie went with him to the clinic at the local Veteran's Administration Hospital. After an exam and several tests the doctors announced to Mattie that her

"Brownie Boy" had lung cancer. The doctors thought they could remove the cancerous lung and he could continue on living with just one lung.

The surgery went quickly but it was discovered there was cancer in both lungs. They completed the surgery without removing his lung. The doctors told Mattie the bad news. They gave him three months to live. Mattie was not having any of that negativity. She asked the doctors not to tell him he had only three months to live. Mattie wanted him to believe he still had one good lung now and he would be fine. Some people thought Mattie made the wrong decision not telling him, but she did it so he would fight.

William did fight as three months turned into six. It looked like he might be winning his battle with cancer. However somewhere around the eighth month, he started weakening. His persistent cough worsened. William Brown passed away in August of 1969 after a gallant nine-month fight.

As William accurately predicted, his family descended on Mattie like vultures; even before he was buried. They demanded to make all the funeral arrangements. They wanted both his belongings and his money. Mattie informed them she was married to him, so they backed off for the short term.

During the days they backed off they researched for a marriage license. Of course, they came up empty in Missouri because their wedding was in Oklahoma. At the funeral there was quiet rumbling and threats about what they might do if Mattie took the veteran's flag. Once again, my male cousins jumped in and protected Mattie by forming a human shield around her at the funeral. A teary Mattie accepted the neatly folded American flag on behalf of a grateful nation.

I believe Mattie met the true love of her life, Charles, in the 1940s in Arkansas. He was enamored with Mattie. Mattie gave him the cold shoulder in the beginning, but eventually his good heart won her over. They dated for three years. Finally, he popped the question and asked her to marry him. Mattie said no. She refused because he was younger than she by five years. Mattie had no other good reason except their age difference of five years. The couple went their separate ways a year later.

Charles and Mattie bumped into each other years later in Kansas City. Again, he tried to woo her into his arms. She let him know she was seeing someone else and married John Littlejohn.

When her marriage to John ended, she called Charles. She was happy to know he was available and the two started dating again. Charles was always supportive of her ambitions. He encouraged her to strive for a higher position at Macy's. Again, Charles asked Mattie to marry him. He told her he loved her. He simply could not continue in limbo. He received a good job offer in Chicago and he wanted to take her with him as his wife. Charles wanted Mattie to make a decision. He told her this was the last time he would ask. Mattie asked for a few days to consider his proposal. They agreed to get back together. A couple days later Charles asked Mattie for her decision.

She told him no a second time and he said goodbye.

Mattie stood there crying, watching him walk out of her life.

After a few years in Chicago, Charles finally married a woman he met there. They stayed married until his wife's death many years later. He and his wife talked with Mattie on the phone occasionally after she married my father John. They talked about their respective kids, the weather and other niceties.

Over the years, Mattie talked with me about Charles. I could tell she still loved him deeply. When Charles' wife died, he moved back to Kansas City to live with his kids. Toward the end of Mattie's life, they stayed in touch.

After Mattie finally passed away, I called him using the number I found in her belongings. I told him she died a short time ago. There was a silent pause. Then I heard Charles gently sobbing. His daughter took the phone away and I told her what happened. Mattie was buried by the time I found his phone number. He was devastated he never got to say goodbye.

☆　　☆　　☆

Life Lessons

Many people have a void inside them due to *father hunger*. This hunger has an enormous impact on how they live their lives.

Like millions of other children, Mattie was a victim of *father hunger*. It's the result of too little intimacy, affection and warmth between a father and a child.

A daughter's first love is found in her father. In Mattie's case it was her grandfather. After he died when she was five, she felt somehow he abandoned her. She also was abandoned by her biological father with whom she didn't form a relationship until mid-life. In addition, there was no love from her step-father.

Mattie's unquenched thirst for father left a deep void in her heart. It's an injury only a father or surrogate father can quench. Mattie went through life feeling much like an orphan.

Security: Orphans need security. A child's most basic need is love and security. Mattie's husband Robert was her first security blanket. He was older and took her in when she had nowhere else to live. He was her protection from the outside world. Mattie always found security in older men. Each time she married for love it was to older men. She never married Charles, the man she truly loved, because he was younger. As a result, he did not represent a father image. In her mind, a younger man meant less security.

Self Esteem: Orphans lack self-esteem. Mattie never felt attractive and loved by her father or her step-father. Her grandfather was the only male figure who made her feel special. He abandoned her—through death—when she was still a little girl. Mattie continued using the men she married to make her feel better about herself. Robert and John Littlejohn were both well-liked men in the community. Marriage to those men was quite a feat for her. When she married John she suddenly had a large, built in, well-known family.

My father John was not well-known, but he made up for it with stability and ambition, things she lacked with John Littlejohn. When they met he had just moved up to the position of Meat Inspector. This was considered an excellent job for a Negro male back in the 1950s. She knew she looked good on his arm.

Survival: Orphans have a way of turning to survival techniques. Mattie tried to rise up from her loneliness and made a decision to take care of herself. She felt she had to because her father figures did not provide that for her. She learned over the years how to take the best advantage of any situation. Whatever would temper her sense of vulnerability, she would do it.

Getting past it: Mattie finally reconciled with her father. However, she was about 50 years old at the time. He had a wife and other grown children. They had less than five years together to make up for a lifetime of his absence. By then her patterns, beliefs and behaviors were deeply entrenched. My Grandfather rescued her from the *love bandit*. If only he had rescued her earlier as a child.

Mattie's feelings of abandonment could have been worked through if she had a loving, understanding partner throughout her life. However, she gradually recognized she had *father issues*. If you have the opportunity or the possibility to reconcile with the parent who abandoned you in your early years, do so. Whether you do or don't reconcile with your father, it's probably a good idea to seek the help of a therapist.

I finally overcame my abandonment issues, however, not until I was an adult woman. I am now ready to dream again and believe in the magic of those dreams.

★ ★ ★

BODY TEMPLE

"The way you think, the way you behave, the way you eat, can influence your life by 30 to 50 years."— Deepak Chopra

I remember the words spoken by the ER doctor. He said, "Mrs. Brown, I don't know how you're still alive!" Mattie's blood pressure reading was an astounding 240/180.

Mattie had been feeling poorly for a couple days. When I talked to her on the phone on the second day, she insisted she wasn't bad enough for a trip to the emergency room. On the third day Mattie told me she was experiencing prolonged bouts of dizziness, nausea, and vomiting. When I insisted she go to the Emergency Room, she balked again. This time I refused to take no for an answer. I jumped in the car to drive over.

I arrived to find Mattie still in her pajamas. She was barely able to get out of bed. Mattie had more than 100 pounds of weight on me, but we managed to slowly make it to my car. The motion of the car added to her nausea. I had to stop the car twice in the two block drive over to the hospital to let Mattie open the door and vomit.

We arrived and, thankfully, a Security Officer and a Registered Nurse brought out a wheelchair to help me get

Mattie inside. We sat in the waiting room for about ten minutes before she was taken to an examining room. Her body was wobbly as she was moved from the wheelchair to the exam table. Just that small amount of movement sent the nurse scrambling for a trash can for Mattie to vomit a third time. Once she calmed down a bit, the nurse took her vitals. I saw a stunned look on the nurse's face after she took Mattie's blood pressure, though she revealed nothing more.

The nurse told us the doctor would be in shortly. Within seconds of the nurse's exit, a doctor appeared. He took Mattie's blood pressure, too. We were glad to see it was a familiar Family Practice doctor from the hospital clinic. He gave us the frightening news. Mattie's blood pressure was so high they weren't sure how she was still alive. She was promptly hooked up to an IV tube and given massive doses of intravenous medicine. The doctor told us she needed to stay in the emergency room until her blood pressure came down. This took four hours. When Mattie was released she was given specific instructions. "Mattie you need to watch your sodium intake. I'm also increasing the dosage of your high blood pressure medicine. And, I want you to take potassium tablets for four weeks."

Mattie was fortunate. Strokes as a result of hypertension led to the untimely death of most of her siblings. Her pre-disposition for hypertension could be traced back to birth. The women in Mattie's family were called *healthy*. Healthy in the sense they were plus-size women with *weight issues*. Their overweight or obesity stemmed from years of high-fat and sodium-rich foods.

As with other women of her generation, Mattie learned to cook at an early age. She loved helping her grandmother prepare all the meals. They did not have refrigerators at home so she retrieved perishable items like milk, cheese, and butter from the cellar. Since she lived on a farm, she also picked fresh fruits and vegetables from the fields. Mattie would sit at the table and her Grandmother allowed her to mix ingredients together. Some seasonings were picked fresh. Her grandmother carefully explained how to incorporate them into their meals. A great deal of time and care went into preparing each meal. Mattie was taught whatever portion size was on your plate you must eat everything. You must clean your plate. That clean plate also let the cook know she did a good job. Most of the day was spent cleaning up after one meal and then beginning to prepare the next.

✿ ☆ ✿ ☆ ✿ ☆ ✿

After the death of Mattie's grandparents, she returned to live with her Mother. Naturally, she was required to help with the cooking. Meals became even more significant because there was a large, hardworking family to feed. As a sharecropper, Mattie learned how to prepare food in quantity, not so much quality.

When Mattie grew up and worked for a wealthy family, she learned to use additional spices and seasoning. While living at their house, the Missus also introduced Mattie to the art of food presentation. "Even the worst-tasting foods can become better and more appetizing with proper presentation," the Missus said. Eventually Mattie took her cooking skills to a bigger audience in Arkansas and finally to Kansas City.

Mattie's *big* family included her spouse, my brother Robert, her mother, siblings, and a host of nieces and nephews. They enjoyed every meal and every important event centered around plenty of food. I remember Sunday dinners, holidays, and reunions where food was the central attraction of the celebration. The dining room table or picnic table filled with everything from ham and ribs to collard greens seasoned with ham hocks. The table was always full of delicious food that was part of family gatherings as well as neighborhood celebrations and get-togethers.

As a child, I remember intimate Sunday dinners with just the two of us. I can still hear Mattie telling me to not forget to sprinkle paprika on the potato salad and the deviled eggs. Not only was the food delicious, but the presentation always made me want to eat more. Mattie always set the table as if we were having guests. There were lovely floral centerpieces with a few grapevines trailing down the center of the table. Even our dinner plates were garnished with a little parsley or another type of greenery.

Unfortunately, the way Mattie prepared food eventually caught up with her. She was in her 50s when the doctor informed her she had acute hypertension or high blood pressure. Mattie probably inherited the condition but was just now showing serious symptoms. Her lifestyle finally brought the disease front and center.

Like most African-Americans, Mattie did not always have quality health insurance. When they went to a doctor, they didn't always receive the proper healthcare or medication. Mattie always made sure I went to the doctor, but she was lax about going herself.

Always ahead of her time, at 62, after yet another bad report from the doctor, Mattie made her declaration. "I'm going on a low sodium diet." She asked her doctor for a recommendation of a dietitian. Armed with a strict list of foods and the amount of sodium she could consume each day, Mattie and I shopped together every weekend. We checked the nutrition labels on food items and often were disappointed. Most of the foods she loved, and she thought were healthy like V8 Juice and canned soup, were loaded with sodium.

Mattie persevered as always. With her same characteristic drive and tenacity, she re-taught herself the art of cooking using better spices and seasonings. I remember the first time she cooked collard greens without ham hocks or salt pork. The greens tasted awful and had to be thrown out. Mattie discovered "No Salt" the salt substitute. After a few more tries, she perfected a collard green recipe that was not only edible but tasted good. It was not as tasty as the former version, but good nevertheless. Mattie found new ways of cooking just about everything.

Watching her sodium intake paid off big for Mattie with a dramatic weight loss. In the beginning, Mattie's weight was about 245-250 lbs. Each month Mattie saw her efforts paying off.

She would call me with updates. "Baby, guess what? I'm at 223."

"I'm so proud of you mom" I encouraged her.

"Just wait, I'm going to get below 200 pounds," she said. She was determined to win this battle.

A year after starting her low sodium diet I received a phone call.

"I DID IT! I DID IT!" Mattie screamed.

"What Mattie? What?" I was busy with my own life and had forgotten this was the day she was scheduled to see her doctor for her annual checkup.

"I finally dropped below 200 pounds. I'm proud to say I weigh 197." Mattie was bursting with excitement. She told me she couldn't remember the last time she weighed less than 200 pounds. By the time of her death, Mattie weighed about 140 pounds. Even with Mattie's dramatic weight loss she still had hypertension. It wasn't as high, but it was still above normal.

Like many African Americans, Mattie was a victim of both nature and nurturing. Nature or heredity plays a big part in the ongoing epidemic of hypertension in the African-American community; especially in women. Mattie's mother, father, and sibling all suffered from hypertension.

By nurturing, I refer to the way Mattie was taught to cook and eat. Yes, the food tasted great, but it had little nutritional value. Mattie and her family cooked and ate a diet high in animal fat and salt their entire lives. Brisket, steak, pork chops, ham and ribs are all loaded with saturated fats. Then they would add sauces, gravies or glazes to everything. Yes, there were vegetables on the table. However, most were seasoned with animal fat like bacon drippings. Dessert could be considered a work of art, with elaborate pie crust and dough strips. They were not only pretty to look at, but they had to taste good as well. It was often a competition between different family members.

The family's hypertension later triggered other conditions. These include diabetes, heart disease, and strokes. All of these conditions, in whole and in part, lead to the premature deaths of Mattie's parents and her siblings. Mattie believed in the magic. She knew she could do whatever she was determined to do.

I believe Mattie's dietary changes added additional years to her life. She was the oldest of her siblings and yet the last to die.

☆　　☆　　☆

Life Lessons:

My Brother and I were lucky. We did not experience problems with hypertension, heart disease, diabetes or strokes. Yes, we grew up eating and loving that down-home Southern cooking, but it didn't seem to affect us. We were both born with thin framed bodies, and never had to worry about weight issues.

Growing up, I was never terribly interested in cooking. It wasn't until I was an adult and was forced to either learn or starve that I finally began to cook. When I began cooking on my own, I was not drawn to Southern cooking. I saved that for visits to Mattie's house. I just cooked the basics: oatmeal or bacon and eggs for breakfast. Lunch might be a sandwich and fruit or one of those frozen dinners. Dinner included a serving of meat and two vegetables. My average adult weight was 125 pounds. All that worked for years.

When I started approaching my 50s, I did start noticing a gradual weight gain. My weight slowly climbed to 135, then 140 and landed on 155. I did not want to suffer the same fate as most of my family members. Currently, I am developing a healthy eating program that I am confident will help not only me, but others as well.

Hypertension: According to The Center for Disease Control (CDC), one in three U.S. adults; an estimated 68 million people; have high blood pressure. The CDC states that African-Americans develop high blood pressure more often and at an earlier age, than the general population. Among African-Americans, women are more likely to have the condition than men.

Diabetes: Hypertension is an important risk factor for diabetes. African-Americans are two times more likely to develop diabetes than the general populations. A whopping 14.7 percent of all African-Americans age 20 or older have diabetes. The CDC data shows that blacks are disproportionately affected by diabetes. The highest numbers for diabetes are among African-American women.

Heart Disease: Heart disease is the leading cause of death for people of most ethnicities in the United States, including African-Americans. However, because African-Americans have so many of the risk factors for heart disease, hypertension, and diabetes, the probability for heart disease increases.

Strokes: The National Stroke Association states that African-Americans are twice as likely to die from stroke as Caucasian-Americans. The rate of first ever strokes in African-Americans is almost doubles that of Caucasians. Strokes also tend to occur earlier in life for African-Americans than Caucasians. Why? Some risk factors play a major role. African-Americans have a higher rate of hypertension and diabetes.

★　　★　　★

SUNSET

"The connection with my Mattie will never be broken because of her physical death. We just communicate differently. The love we have is impossible to break. It's the most powerful connection in the universe. As long as mom and I exist now and forever the connection will stay."

A ray of light burst through the window in Mattie's corner room at Trinity Lutheran Hospital. It lightly brushed the foot of her bed. How strange, I thought, its pouring rain outside. At that moment, a commercial for Chevy trucks came on. As the song "Like a Rock" played, I turned to her. "Mom, there's your song!" I said excitedly. There was no response. The moment of excitement quickly faded as I realized I might never see her snap her fingers and bob her head to that song again.

I sank down in my chair seated next to her bed and stared at her. I talked to her, pleading with her, to get better quickly so I could take her home with me. I felt anger well up inside. I was angry at myself and one person I entrusted with her care.

Rewind

I walked into Mattie's new two-bedroom apartment and had to laugh. It looked like a jungle in there. Mattie always had a green thumb, so the living room was filled with live plants, baskets of flowers, vines growing along the window and even a couple artificial trees. The two-bedroom apartment came with her new position as manager of Rosedale Towers, a senior citizens high-rise in Kansas City, KS.

When Mattie first moved into Rosedale Towers it was strictly as a resident. However, she wanted to generate extra income, so she took the job of security guard for the building on the weekends. She basically sat at the front entrance and made everyone sign in upon entering. With the increase of technology—in the form of ID badge operated doors at her job was eliminated.

When the Manager's job became available, residents urged her to apply. Mattie was very much a people person. The residents said she was kind and generous. At first she backed off from the idea, using all kind of excuses. Finally, she surrendered and, in 1980, Mattie Brown was named Manager of Rosedale Towers. In that position, Mattie would attend city and state functions. I remember her excitement about buying a dress to attend the Governor's Ball.

In the years that followed I got married, gave birth to a daughter, and got divorced. My divorce seemed especially hard on Mattie. She was relaxed in knowing I was married and she had a grandchild. Now that I was divorced with the responsibility for a small child, she worried about me.

Several times I had to take her to the Emergency Room (ER) due to her high blood pressure. I remember one doctor telling us she had "a strong constitution."

"Your blood pressure was 240/180 when you came in here. I don't know how you are alive!" the doctor in the ER room said. Mattie sometimes forgot to take her blood pressure medicine, or sometimes she didn't take it the way it was prescribed. She complained it was making her sick. As we left the ER the physician asked us to follow up with her primary doctor. I went to the doctor with Mattie to make sure she told her doctor everything. He changed her prescriptions, but I still was not convinced she would stick to her 'doctor's orders'.

In 1988, I started noticing a difference in Mattie. When I entered her apartment, the jungle of thriving plants and flowers was no more. Most of her plants and flowers had died. When I asked her what happened to them, she told me she was tired of trying to keep up so many plants. Her work as manager started to slip. She told me her boss was coming to see her to talk about her work. I was worried because she had always been bragged upon for her exemplary work. Mattie said she thought he was being over critical. I was deeply concerned.

In early 1989, I convinced Mattie to give up her job knowing her boss would ask her to leave sooner than later. I knew she would feel humiliated. Reluctantly, she became solely a resident again.

I was so concerned I took her to several doctors. The doctors told me, "Well, she is at that age. They just start to forget things. It's a part of the aging process." Frustrated, someone told me to take her to a Gerontologist. I never heard of that type of specialist before. Fortunately, they had a Gerontology Center at Kansas University Medical Center two blocks away from Mattie's apartment. I made an appointment.

My cousin Janet and I accompanied Mattie. After conducting some tests, they came back with answers. Finally, someone with a straight answer I thought.

I was not prepared for what they were about to tell me, nor did I fully understand it. Janet and I were called into the conference room where two doctors were sitting, along with Mattie. I prepared myself for the worst, thinking perhaps Mattie had a brain tumor.

The doctor said, "There is no easy way to tell you this, but she has Alzheimer's Disease." I spaced out and could not recall anything the doctor said after that. I remembered hearing the word before; Alzheimer's. But I was unsure of what it meant. There was much less information available about the disease in 1989.

"What is Alzheimer's Disease?" I wondered. Were there pills available to make her better? Was it even possible for her to get better?

When the doctor stopped talking, he looked at me and said, "It's alright if you want to cry."

I didn't say anything. I thought, why would I cry? Did I miss something? Is it a brain tumor? I looked at Mattie and a concerned look crossed her face. I grabbed her hand and held it tightly. My cousin Janet showed no emotion. I hoped Janet understood what was going on because I didn't understand, nor could I stay focused.

We left Kansas University Medical Center and returned to Mattie's apartment to sit and talk.

Mattie kept saying she did not want to be put in a home. "I don't want to be lead around like I'm crazy."

Thankfully, Janet processed everything that happened and comforted Mattie. "Aunt Mattie," she explained, "The doctors said nothing should change right now. Let's just take this one day at a time." We sat around and talked about a lot of things.

Mattie started laughing and I knew she would be okay. Janet and I left her apartment late in the afternoon. Once outside, I had to know just what we were up against. "What does all this mean?" I asked. She instructed me to read the informational brochures they gave me and to research Alzheimer's.

I did and the more I read, the more I sank into a depression. I was a single mother with a small child, how could I get through this? I managed; one day at a time.

❀ ❀ ❀

Mattie was assigned a Social Worker and a home care nurse to check on her once a month. As she slowly declined, the doctor visits became more frequent, and the nurse checked in on her biweekly. I tried to balance the independence Mattie so desperately craved while keeping her safe.

I took away her car keys and her car after a five-minute drive to the supermarket turned into a one hour-long 'adventure'. Mattie would wear the same clothes two or even three times in a row, whether they were clean or dirty.

The scariest moments were when she walked away. One time I came to pick her up and she was nowhere to be found. I frantically drove around the neighborhood in a panic searching, searching, and searching. Mattie was nowhere to be found, so I drove back to her apartment, hoping she would there. She was still gone! I looked up to see a van pull in the back and Mattie climbed out.

I went running to back door of the high rise where the van was dropping her off. "Mom, who was that and where have you been?"

"I just went to see some friends at Rainbow Towers" Mattie replied with a smile.

"What friends Mom, and who was just dropped you off?" I asked in an alarmed, motherly tone.

Well, that tone did not set well with Mattie. She promptly reminded me I was the daughter and she was the mother. She could go out and see whoever she wanted without telling me. I backed off and explained I was there to pick her up as we had discussed. And that I became worried when she wasn't there.

Mattie's response, "Oh well, I forgot. Let's go now. Where were we going again?"

In 1991, I got the phone call I was dreading from her Social Worker. She let me know she had conversations with the doctors and nurses treating Mattie. They concluded it was time to make some decisions regarding Mattie's living arrangements. The doctor wanted Mattie and I to get together and discuss options.

I talked with Mattie and she sounded strangely childlike when she asked me not to send her to a home for crazy people. She said, "You know, like you see in the movies. You're in a padded room and nurses lead you everywhere, even the bathroom." I reassured her I wouldn't let that happen.

As we arrived at the doctor's office to discuss options, a knot grew in my stomach. I expressed Mattie's wishes to the doctors. She wanted to stay independent as along as possible. I turned to Mattie and asked her if she wanted to live with me, or in an assisted living apartment. She jumped at the assistant living, reiterating her desire to be independent. The doctor said the Social Worker would work on it, however her choices were limited based on Mattie's income. I assured the doctor I would visit each and every place. There was no way I could let her live in just any old place.

I talked to my cousin Janet and other family members about the decision that had to be made.

My cousin George was a minster. Every Sunday morning he picked Mattie up at her apartment to take her to church on Sundays. He told me he had an idea. "Why not have Aunt Mattie come live with me?"

I told George she could live with me, but she wanted to stay independent.

He said, "Look, my wife Alma is retired and her mother lives there, too. I think Aunt Mattie would enjoy having someone her age to talk with. After all, they've known each other 40 years."

I told him I would talk to Mattie, but I did not think she wanted to live with anybody. Later that day I talked with Mattie. She was hesitant, so I told her to think about it.

While we were waiting to get a list of assisted living apartments, unbeknownst to me, George talked to Mattie after I did. He must have been pretty persuasive, because she finally agreed to stay with him.

The next time I talked to Mattie she told me, "I want to live with George and Alma."

I said "Okay, but if you don't like it we'll come up with something else."

It was the worst mistake I ever made. I'm sure George's suggestion for Mattie to stay with him came straight from his heart. I think he sincerely thought it would be the best thing for her. However, I feel George never truly considered how his wife, Alma, felt about the situation. As an afterthought, I wish now I would have stopped the move from going forward when I first became aware of Alma's disdain.

When I went over to George and Alma's house, they were preparing a room for Mattie. Alma had to give up her office space to make this happen. I stood in the doorway as she was cleaning and said, "Wow! You're working hard!" There was so much clutter in that room, I knew it would take her awhile to clean everything.

She snapped back at me, "I want you to know I'm not happy about this."

I backed up, telling her I would come back when George got home.

The next day I reached George and told him about the conversation I had with Alma the day before. I told him it wasn't too late to rearrange things—I hadn't got the list of assisted living apartments yet.

He said, "Don't mind Alma. She's just mad; she finally had to clean out that room. She wants her there as much as I do." I believed him. That was truly my mistake.

The process of moving Mattie in with George and Alma was extremely tough on me. Mattie seemed to take it all in stride. After Mattie moved her lighter belongings over to George and Alma's, I went through her things. As I looked around her room I felt a deep sense of loss. I curled up in her bed in a semi-fetal position and cried. I knew our lives would never be the same.

I searched through her closet and noticed half her clothes were gone and she had only a couple pair of shoes. I think she forgot her clothes in the washing machine. The Building Manager probably did not know who they belonged to and threw them away. When I found her shoes in plastic trash bags,

I figured she probably threw them down the trash shoot by mistake.

Mattie's large furniture items were divided between me and what she could take with her to George and Alma's. The apartment was finally empty. I stood and looked around at the bare walls one last time. I heard a family member call my name, but I didn't answer. It seemed no one understood I needed a little time to process everything.

The next week I bought Mattie five new dresses. I tried to buy her some shoes. However, her sizes 12 wide feet were hard to fit. I brought the dresses to her and she was happy. She tried on each dress and walked as if she was a fashion runway model.

Juggling it all was a challenge: Mattie on the weekends; an active six-year-old daughter; a full-time job; a fiancé; and a new home. Sometimes I fell short. Occasionally, every weekend with Mattie turned into every other weekend. Mattie was usually busy with the church where my cousin George ministered. For a while, she also attended adult daycare. We relished the weekends she spent with me.

Eventually, Mattie experienced increasingly dramatic mood swings. Sometimes she was happy, other times depressed. When she went through her depressed phases she did not want to eat. I had to pump her with Ensure supplements and her favorite canned peaches. Her weight dropped dramatically. She once weighed over 200 pounds; now she was a slim 140 pounds. Sometimes we enjoyed excellent conversations, other times her memory was spotty and off track.

Gradually, her depression lingered longer and longer until eventually she didn't seem to snap out of it.

One weekend, she told me she did not like living with George and Alma.

"Why mom?" I asked, "You seem to be a busy lady, sometimes too busy for me."

"Alma tells everyone you don't want me. It hurts my feelings." Mattie replied.

"Mom, are sure? Sometimes you get things mixed up."

"No, I'm not. Alma tells everybody on the phone, at church, the mailman. Even the mall man," Mattie said.

"What is the mall man, Mattie?"

"The man that stands at the mall!" she replied, as if I was crazy for not knowing.

I did not take her seriously at first because she had things so mixed up. I mean, what kind of person would say that? After all Alma was a Minster's wife.

"Mattie, do you want to stay with me?" I asked her.

She said, "No I want to live by myself again."

The next weekend I decided to do something I hoped would be special for her. When I was a little girl, Mattie always took me to a special lookout area to watch the airplanes land at the airport. I was fascinated by the planes and she could see the joy in my face, so we made the trip often. We would pack a lunch or sometimes we would just stop for ice cream. It was our special place.

My daughter and I picked her up and I drove to our favorite lookout spot. While driving I kept our destination a secret, and along the way we stopped to get burgers.

We arrived and a big smile spread over Mattie's face. I was relieved to see she remembered our place. The airport was now used just for small or private planes, but it was still busy. We got out our burgers and ate them as we sat near a small stone wall. When we were finished, I scraped together some coins from my purse to put in the viewer so we could look closer at the planes as they landed on the runway. Mattie and I acted like kids again, excited about every plane landing. We probably spent at least a couple of hours there.

As we walked backed to the car, Mattie looked at me and said, "This is the best day of my life." I'm not sure who had the biggest silly grin after that, she or I.

The next weekend was Labor Day, 1992. I planned to take a trip with my then-fiancé. My seven-year-old daughter was spending the weekend with her father. Still, everything that could possibly go wrong with my plans went wrong. Finally, I told my fiancé it was not meant for me to go this weekend. "Nothing has gone right; there are so many road blocks. I don't know why, but it's just not meant for me to travel." Mattie always told me that God sometimes puts up roadblocks to keep you safe.

That Saturday before Labor Day I did the usual chores, washing clothes and cleaning the house. Despite an allergy flare-up from dust developing into a full-blown sinus headache, I went to the store. I couldn't wait to return home, relax and nurse my headache. Once home, I put the groceries away and settled into Mattie's favorite chair. I was just getting cozy when there was a knock at the door. My fiancé opened the door to find my cousin George Jr. It was a long time since I had seen him, so I jumped up and hugged him. He hugged me tight and held on a little longer than usual.

When he released me he said, "Rae, I have bad news."

"What?" I asked, my voice quivering.

"Aunt Mattie is at the hospital. She's had a massive stroke."

I let out an ear-piercing scream. "Is she alive?"

"Yes, she is. Or, she was when I left," George said.

I kept repeating, "Oh God, oh God, please keep her alive!"

151

My fiancé helped me find my purse and get organized. I called my cousin Janet, who truly my rock throughout Mattie sickness. I asked her to meet me at the hospital. My fiancé and I jumped in the car and sped to the hospital. I sobbed all the way, praying for her to stay alive, at least until I could see her.

We arrived at the hospital and I jumped out of the car. I ran to the elevator and up to her floor. I saw the waiting room with family members.

I ran through the door. "Is mom okay?"

Alma was the first to approach me. "I wondered IF you were coming."

"Of course I was coming," I fired back. I was too upset to process the implications of what Alma said. Fortunately, the doctor in the waiting room brought me up to speed.

Mattie was at the hospital with Alma visiting Alma's mother. Mattie and Alma were eating a meal in the hospital cafeteria when Mattie complained about her head hurting, "really bad." The next moment, she collapsed onto the table.

A Code Blue was called and Mattie had a brain scan. She had a brain aneurysm that burst in her head. The doctors needed my permission to operate to relieve the pressure from the fluid on her brain. "Yes, give me the forms," I told him immediately. "And when can I see my mother?"

The doctors went to get the paperwork as I waited outside. The negative energy, what if's, in the waiting room was too much for me. So I stood in the hall next to the waiting room. I needed to stay positive. I couldn't believe Mattie's situation was deteriorating so fast.

My cousin Janet arrived with my fiancé. She asked me, "Why are you waiting out here?" I told her the situation and they both held me while I cried softly.

The nurse came out to get me and take me back to the area where they were keeping her. The doctor, the nurse, and I were in a small cramped office. He went over the release forms and explained that the surgery they would perform tonight was to drain the fluid off her brain. He assured me that Mattie was stable enough for them to do the surgery. I asked when I could see her and was told I could see her in a few moments, but only two people at a time could go in her room.

Finally, I went in to see Mattie. If I didn't know what had just happened to her, I would never have known anything was wrong. She was awake and talking but didn't remember anything. I left the room so other family members could see her but returned again. It was hard to hold back my tears but seeing her in good spirits made it easier. I left again when the nurse came to take her for more testing and to shave her head in preparation for the surgery.

I sat in a small area room close to her room. I was still keeping myself far away from family, though my fiancé and cousin Janet stayed with them. Alone, I could reflect on what was happening and have a good cry. I was joined by the primary physician of Alma's mother, Dr. Smith. I looked up at her with my nose running and eyes puffy from crying.

She asked me, "Do you feel guilty about abandoning your Mother?"

I said loudly, "Oh my God, mom knew what she was talking about and I didn't believe her." In fact, Alma was telling everyone within earshot that Mattie was living in their house because I didn't want her.

How could anyone be that cruel? I thought.

I explained to Dr. Smith what really happened. I'm not sure if she believed me, as she switched the conversation to a more positive subject.

Dr. Smith said, "When your Mother gets better, I want to examine her. I don't think she has Alzheimer's. I think she may be having mini strokes."

I kept this potentially positive news close to my heart. I did not comfort Alma or George. I had to focus on sending positive energy and prayer to Mattie as she went into surgery. I would need that energy to counter the doctor's assessment of Mattie's odds. Dr. Rama told me Mattie had a three percent chance of surviving the surgery, which would close the base of the aneurysm with a clip, and recovery.

I tried to stay positive though my thoughts swung wildly. Mattie had beaten the odds in so many ways her entire life, I was sure she would surprise everyone again. Then, the scared little girl inside me came out. I did not want to be an orphan. Yet, with the next thought, I was confident there had to be a good reason her aneurysm burst in a hospital. If it happened in any other place she would have died already. Surely that meant she was supposed to live and recover. Again, I began to pray for Mattie and for me to have the strength to stay positive. Tonight was to be the first battle of this war.

Surgery was scheduled for 7:30 p.m. I walked around the Intensive Care Unit (ICU) to find Dr. Rama asleep behind the nurses' station. His pillow was against the wall and he seemed oblivious to everything around him. I smiled and thought how grateful I was for his dedication and that of the other surgeons. What a burden it must be to hold the lives of others in your hands every day!

As the time drew nearer they let me see Mattie again. She was fast asleep and snoring really loud.

"Mom, I love you," I whispered softly.

She said, "Love you too," though still sleeping lightly.

My cousin George joined Mattie and I for a prayer near her bed. After the prayer, the nurse told us it was time to take her into surgery. I gave Mattie a kiss on the cheek as we were given directions to the surgical waiting room. I felt weak and leaned on my fiancé. Suddenly I remembered I hadn't eaten anything since morning. He asked if I wanted something. All the choices were from the vending machine. "No, I don't think I could keep anything down," I replied. Thank God Alma had left earlier. Together, with my cousins Janet, George, and my fiancé and at the hospital we began the vigil.

It seemed like forever, but finally Dr. Rama appeared in the waiting room and told us everything went well. He said early the next day they had scheduled an angioplasty. This would be followed by the life or death surgery. For now, Mattie was returned to her room.

Once back in her room, I got to see her for the first time since the surgery. I took a deep breath, not knowing what I would find. My first glimpse of Mattie coming in the door was of her head wrapped in bandages with a tube coming out of head, which was draining bloody fluid.

"Mom?" I said.

She turned her head a little to look at me and managed a weak smile. I sat next to her bed and did most of the talking. Mattie said she still didn't understand how she got herself into this mess. That's my mom, I thought, still upbeat. We all left with the satisfaction of knowing that Mattie was doing well.

I remember it was a beautiful September Sunday morning. The previous night they told us Mattie's angioplasty would be performed at 7:30 a.m. My fiancé and I raced to get to the hospital in time. We got there only to discover they had wheeled her into surgery early and she was already in the middle of the procedure.

Honestly, it was scariest day of my life thus far. The whole family had arrived, including cousins I had not seen in a while. Dr. Rama explained the six-hour surgical procedure to me in layman terms. He told me the most important thing Mattie had going for her now was her tenacity.

I smiled, "Yes that would sure describe my mom."

After the surgery, we were only permitted to see her two at a time, and only for a few minutes. I let everyone go ahead because George and I needed to be last.

Before I could pry Mattie's hospital door open I could hear her snoring. I spoke to her, but this time she didn't wake up. I know she knew we were there. George and I prayed. That prayer was a "shake the church prayer." I felt a loving energy all around the room. I knew God was in charge and there would be a divine intervention. I kissed her and told I would see her when she woke up.

George Sr. left with most of the family to give his Sunday sermon. Before he left he gave me the direct number to call as soon as we got word.

The remaining family members gathered in the surgery waiting room, with a few cousins taking food orders. I felt so confident that the divine light was on Mattie that I not only ate, but also managed to sleep for a couple hours.

As Dr. Rama and the others doctors finally emerged through the waiting room door, we all stood.

"It went very well; much better than I expected," he said with his Indian accent. A loud cheer went up by family members. The other doctors came in to congratulate Dr. Rama on his success. Another doctor stayed past his shift just to see the outcome of the surgery. I knew Dr. Rama was a brilliant doctor, but I also knew a second set of divine hands had been there in the operating room. Dr. Rama explained Mattie would be in recovery for a few more hours before we could see her.

I immediately called George's church. Alma picked the phone up immediately.

"Moms out of surgery and everything went better than expected."

"Thank God," she said. "George has been so upset." She told me as soon as church was out they would drive back to the hospital. My next phone call was to my ex-husband to let my daughter know her Granny was okay.

I knew George was genuinely upset. Mattie was the matriarch in the family. Not only that, but he was one of my first cousins who were the close part of my brother's crew. I believe one of his missions after my brother Robert's death was to take care of Mattie and I. I was told by a family member that the sermon that morning at church was about the power of prayer. George cried through most of the prayer.

During the service, Alma was perched by the phone in the back of the small church. George and Alma had a signal worked out that she would give him from the back to let him know everything was okay. As soon as the okay was given by Alma the church erupted in a joyous celebration; the way only a Pentecostal Church fellowship can do.

When I finally went in to see Mattie she was groggy. She had a breathing tube but still she looked great considering what she had been through. Mattie was unable to speak to me, but her eyes told me she was okay. Later, more family arrived.

I was exhausted as evening approached. George said he would stay at the hospital at that night. Gratefully, I left and actually slept like a baby all night.

The next day the nurses explained to me the process of weaning Mattie off the ventilator. They thought they could do it that day. Sure enough, Mattie took breaths on her own. She spoke a couple of words at a time. Later in the afternoon, she started speaking in sentences. I left to pick up my daughter from school and tell her the good news.

Later that evening I got a call from George informing me they had to put Mattie's breathing tube back in again.

I heard Alma in the background shouting at me. "You need to come to the hospital and see your mother! She is on a breathing tube!"

Thoroughly pissed off at Alma, I screamed back, "I was there when they took it out!"

I thought why am I trying to have a conversation with this deranged woman? I'm sure George's ears were bleeding. Finally, he told his wife, "She was there when they took the ventilator out." Then he informed me that Mattie's respiratory rates were down and they had to reattach it.

Again, I wished I knew what Alma harbored in her heart. Why was she always making me out to be a monster who hated her mother? Did that happen to her at some point? I will never know the answer.

I took the next day off work to stay with Mattie. The nurses had removed the ventilator again. The nurse told me not to worry, Mattie would be only making good changes now and she suggested I go get something to eat.

Mattie was scheduled to stay in the trauma area for two weeks. She was given three seizure medications; which are standard protocol for this type of brain trauma. A few days later when I came to visit her, Mattie's head was as big as a basketball. The nurse told me she developed an allergic reaction to one of the three seizure medicines; however, they didn't know which one. The doctors decided to remove all the medications and re-introduced them to her one at a time. After a week, her head returned to normal size. The decision was made to leave her on only one seizure medication. The side effects from the powerful drugs were showing up in other ways. She was unable to open her eyes or speak.

Mattie had lots of visitors. A cousin I hadn't seen in many years, my niece Wilma, and her mother Audrey came to the hospital in Kansas City from Houston.

Through everything Mattie still kept her sense of humor.

My niece said to her, "Oh grandma, grandma, grandma."

Mattie's response was, "Hmm hmm hmm."

It was her way of letting us know she was aware of our presence and she heard every word.

Finally, Mattie was moved to a regular floor in the hospital. She had a private room at the end of the hallway. She still could not open her eyes or speak. I brought my seven-year-old daughter to the hospital for the first time. I knew it would make Mattie happy and motivate her to keep fighting. My daughter had her Girl Scout uniform on and Mattie had never seen her in it before. As my daughter stood next to her granny's hospital bed she looked a little frightened.

"Granny can hear you," I reassured my daughter. I told Mattie, "Your baby is here. She's wearing her Girl Scout uniform. Please try to open your eyes and see her." I saw Mattie struggling. She did it! No way would she let her grandbaby down. Mattie turned her head to see her for about ten seconds. Then she closed her eyes and smiled. Then she turned her head back toward the sound of the television.

One evening I came to visit and a nurse was in the room. As soon as I walked in Mattie said, "There's my baby."

I was shocked and jumped for joy. "Mom, you're speaking again!" I called my cousin Janet and told her the good news. I put the phone next to Mattie's ear so Janet could talk to her. The next day she spoke to my daughter on the phone. We were all excited Mattie seemed to be getting better.

However, our joy was shorted lived. Three weeks later I came to visit Mattie thinking I would hear her say a familiar, "Hi baby." I was devastated to learn she had a severe seizure overnight. So severe she now had the mentality of an infant. My world seemed to come crashing down around me. I got close to Mattie and kissed her. She looked back at me with hollow eyes. My heart was breaking. Gathering my thoughts, I asked the doctor and nurse to step outside the room. I asked them not to talk negatively while in my Mattie's room. I kept asking, "What's next? What we can do next?"

The doctors told me IF she made it out of the hospital she would need to be housed in a "facility" with around the clock care. I told them I just couldn't accept that. If Mattie wanted to keep fighting, I was going to fight along with her and she would preferably stay with me.

Each morning I got out of bed and started my day with a call to the nurses' station to check on Mattie. Each day they told me she was stable. I somehow mustered up the strength to go to work. However, I would go through the motions at work in a zombie-like state. Then after work, I would spend two or three hours with Mattie before leaving to pick up my daughter at extended after school care. Finally, I would take her to her Girl Scout meeting or dance class.

On Friday, October 30, my visit with Mattie after work brought me more bad news. The nurse and I stepped outside the Mattie's room. She informed me Mattie had suffered kidney failure. The nurse told me it was only "a matter of time." I told her I would not accept it until Mattie did. I stayed with Mattie for two hours. She was mostly sleeping now. I knew I had to leave to pick up my daughter. This was Halloween weekend and I wanted her to carry on as much as possible her normal life. Her father took her for the weekend so I could spend as much time with Mattie as possible. I went back to the hospital that evening and stayed a few more hours. I watched her monitors and Mattie's heart rate seemed strong, so I felt comfortable leaving for the night.

It was raining hard when I arrive at the hospital early Halloween morning. I stopped by the nurses' station for an update before I entered Mattie's room. I was told nothing had changed. Mattie was putting up a good fight. "Well, yes, that's my mom," I told the nurses at the station.

Mattie's nurse said, "I don't know how she is still alive. Most people go quickly."

I snapped, "Because she's not ready to go. And, as I have said many times, I am not accepting anything until she is ready!"

Once in Mattie's room, I turned on the television and began to talk to her as if it was any other time in our lives. "Mattie today is Halloween and your granddaughter is going to be a ninja turtle." I talked to her about her new dance classes and the latest Girl Scout badge she was working on.

Through the window in Mattie's room, a ray of light appeared just brushing the foot of her bed. It was pouring down rain. How odd, I thought. At that moment the song from the Chevy truck commercial "Like a Rock" came on I turned to Mattie. "Mom there's your song" I said excited. No response. Seated next to her bed I asked her to get better so I could take her home with me.

I felt a hot anger welling up inside me. I was angry at myself and angry at the people who I thought cared and wanted her in their home to nurture her and share her remaining time. I had to fight my negative thoughts about her prognosis. What good would all this negative thinking and negative energy do? It wasn't anybody's fault. No one could have known this enemy was lurking in her brain. I told myself when Mattie got better she would be home with me. There will be more opportunities to smile and laugh while watching planes take off and land.

My cousin Janet came by to visit. She talked to Mattie. I think our goal was to talk to her as if everything was okay. So, we laughed about things from our childhood, things Mattie could understand. The nurse told us there were no significant changes and late that evening we went to our respective homes to sleep and start the next day. I should have stayed at the hospital because I called the nurses' station three times that night and got very little sleep.

Sunday was the same routine. I woke early, though I did not sleep much that night. I grabbed fast food breakfast on the way to the hospital. I stopped at the nurses' station and she said there were no real changes in Mattie's condition. They were just keeping her comfortable.

I was in luck when I caught the doctors as they stopped by to visit Mattie bright and early. He had nothing new to report and just gave me some "doctor jargon" I didn't quite understand.

He told me, "She is a fighter." He asked me a question that stunned me. "Has your mother woken up and talked to you yet?"

I replied, "No."

The doctor detected confusion in my voice. He continued, "Sometimes they wake up and talk to you one last time."

I told the doctor I believed Mattie said all she had to say when she started speaking out of the clear blue a few weeks ago.

The exchange was a strange one from the doctor who had told me the day before that Mattie had the mind of an infant after the seizure.

Sunday ended with Mattie still fighting.

Monday, November 2, 1992

Almost two months passed as Mattie lay in her hospital bed. I called the hospital early that morning. The nurses told me on the phone that Mattie's body was slowly shutting down. They asked me whether to call a Code Blue. I said "yes" but not until I could get there. I told my fiancé, and then I called my cousin Janet and put her on standby. I hurried to drop my daughter off at before school care. I was stilling playing the role of superwoman. Trying to do everything myself.

Arriving at the hospital I drove up and down the aisles of the parking lot. It seemed like I would never find a place to park. Once parked, I walked as fast as I could to the hospital entrance, up the elevator and down the halls to Mattie's room. I reached her room only to find her heart rate jumping all over the place.

My first thought was she was still fighting to maintain her heart rate. The nurse dashed my hopes by telling me it was protein settling around her heart. I watched Mattie's head movements. I was told that she was breathing strictly from her brainstem.

I sat by Mattie's bed trying to carry on a normal conversation. But I had to step out in the hallway a couple times to just cry. I didn't want her to see or hear me crying. From two to three o'clock each afternoon, the lights were dimmed in the unit for quiet time. I left her room to sit in the nearby lobby and catch my breath.

Dr. Smith was now one of Mattie's doctors. She came and sat down next to me. "Your mom is hanging on for you. I've seen it happen many times." Dr. Smith shared with me the stories of other patients who waiting until all the family members were present or waited for them to finally leave before passing.

I told Dr. Smith it was incredibly hard for me to watch Mattie in the condition she was in right now. She gave me a hug and left to make her rounds.

I thought about Dr. Smith's comments. Could it be possible that Mattie continued her fight due to her tenacious spirit this time, not for herself, but because of her granddaughter and me?

All this talk from the doctors and nurses about her having the mind of an infant was probably physical, but spiritually I knew my Mattie was still there. There was still 30 minutes left in quiet time, but I returned to Mattie's room anyway. I sat at her bedside and tried to get the strength to ask her questions. This was hardest thing I ever had to do. Holding her hand, I took a deep breath and asked, "Mom are you fighting because you're a fighter? Or, are you fighting for Crystal and me? I know you're tired." I paused, took another deep breath, and dug deep down in my soul. "Mom if you're tired and you want to go, it's okay. I'm strong like you. Crystal and I will miss you forever, but we will be okay. Do what's best for you."

As I looked at her face she had a peaceful look despite the sound of the brainstem breathing and jerky head movements. I wiped the drool from her mouth and put Vaseline on her ears. Brainstem breathing made them raw from the jerky head movements. "Mom, it hurts so much to see you like this. I don't know what else to do." Then a Bible verse came to mind. It was the first Bible verse she taught me when I was a little girl. Holding her hand again, I closed my eye and began to recite the 23rd Psalm aloud.

The LORD is my shepherd; I shall not want.
He maketh me to lie down in green pastures;
He leadeth me beside the still waters.
He restoreth my soul.
He leadeth me in the paths of righteousness
for His name's sake.
Yea, though I walk through the valley of the
shadow of death, I will fear no evil, for Thou
art with me; Thy rod and thy staff, they
comfort me.
Thou preparest a table before me in the
presence of mine enemies.
Thou anointest my head with oil; my cup
runneth over.

*Surely goodness and mercy shall follow me
all the days of my life, and I will dwell in the
house of the LORD forever.*

And ever.

I heard a ringing sound. "Amen," I finished.

I looked up to see the monitor alarms sounding and the lights flashing. Suddenly the lines went flat. I began sobbing uncontrollably. Instantly I felt a hole rip through my heart.

The nurse entered the room moments later to turn off the monitors. She told me that hearing is the last of the senses to diminish "so keep talking to her." The nurse left the room to give us privacy in these last moments together.

I told mom how much I loved her and would miss her. I thanked her for being such an awesome Mother and inspiring role model.

Another nurse came in and asked me which funeral home to call.

I started sobbing again, creating a communication problem for the nurse. Finally, I wrote down Watkins Funeral Home. We were left alone again.

As I stared into her face she looked so peaceful. I stood up and touched her face, "Mommy I'm going to miss you so much." I felt like an orphan who had just been dropped off on a stranger's doorsteps. I grabbed Mattie's hand, sat back down and buried my head on the side of her bed and cried. Sobbing so hard I had to lift my head to catch my breath. Once again my head was buried into the side of her hospital bed.

Then I felt warmth on the left side of my upper body. I lifted my head to see a ray of light, almost blinding, come through

Mattie's hospital room window. The light brushed the side of Mattie's bed where I was sitting. At the same time I heard the sounds of rain pounding against the glass. I had to get up from where I was seated to see where the light was coming from. I stepped around the light and went over to the window and followed the beam skyward. I traced the light back to the clouds that had a soft, golden glow. I stepped away and stood with my back against the wall. I tried to look at the light but couldn't without squinting.

As I closed my eyes a warm peaceful feeling came over me. All the questions about life and death I had asked the Creator as a child flashed through my mind. I no longer needed to cry; I was at peace. Mattie had fulfilled her destiny on Earth. I knew her spirit left her body in that light and she was finally at peace.

★　　　★　　　★

Life Lessons

Take Time to Heal: The first couple weeks after Mattie's funeral I felt really peaceful. I did not cry. I was strong. When I would talk to her I would say, "See mom, I told you I was strong like you." Then, around the third week, it finally hit me. I really was an orphan. I needed to go through the grieving process. My fiancé became worried about me, but I knew I was alright. I just had to get through this process. Strangely enough, the shower seems to be a place that would trigger a crying spell.

The peace I felt I'm sure had numbed me to the reality. The pain was excruciating. That was followed by the guilt of not believe her when she told me how Alma was treating her. The result of the guilt was anger at Alma and how she was somehow responsible for mom's death. Then I felt depressed and lonely. Everyone thought I should be getting on with my life, but I had to deal with it on my own terms and in my own time.

Eventually, it did get better. Each month I healed a little more. I got through the holidays, her birthday and my own. It took about a year to come full circle and to be able to look to the future again. I was unable to think about Mattie without pain and sadness, but the wrenching pain was gone. As time passed and I more fully healed I was able to fully enjoy my daughter again and focus on the experience of living.

I did not ask for proof of Alzheimer after my Mattie's death. I considered how much her brain had been through and decided against it.

After Mattie's funeral, I asked the creator to eliminate the date Nov 2nd from my psyche. I knew Mattie would not want to be sad and crying when that day approach. I have never remembered that day since. After that day passes, I remember, but it does not have the impact.

Tolerance and forgiveness: It takes a special type of wisdom to be able to tolerate and forgive others. Mattie had instinctively had that ability, and it is something that I am still trying to master. What a beautiful uplifting feeling it must be to have the gift for tolerating and forgiving others. I try to use both tolerance and forgiveness in my everyday life. I learned to let people be who they are. It does not mean I let people walk on me. I just separate myself from them and let them learn their own life lessons. I can only change or control myself.

The months following Mattie's death, I did not see George or Alma very often. I never confronted Alma. Part of me wanted to and I attempted to, but something always stopped me.

Perhaps it was divine intervention. I could hear my Mattie's voice talk to me about forgiveness. How could this compare to what she had to forgive? I know George had done his best. The first Mother's Day after my Mattie's death, he made an unexpected visit. He was there to check up on me. He knew this Mother's Day would be painful for me. His gesture meant a lot to me. George and Alma have both died and I will leave it to the higher power to judge Alma and her actions.

Humble: Dealing with dementia is a humbling experience. To see a once vibrant person reduced to an almost childlike state is painful. Mattie could not remember simple tasks. Things like putting on clean clothes, knowing if she had brushed her teeth, or remembering what she had for lunch. She lived with hallucinations; not knowing if what she saw was real or not. Mattie would fall into bouts of deep depression. Yet she still tried to live with dignity. Now I am humbled by people with disabilities. I look at them differently, almost in amazement. They have been dealt these issues and yet they push on.

When Mattie died, I was still unprepared. I never really believed that my mother, whom I loved so much, the woman who had given me so much and fought so hard, could actually die. I never knew life without her. The world did not seem like the world without my mother.

Appreciative: I have learned to appreciate the little things. My last outing with Mattie was one of the simplest things we could do, and yet, it was the best day of both of our lives. I am more appreciative of those who are still living and therefore am able to move on from a devastating experience; on to a new life full of family and friends.

I am thankful to the Divine Creator for answering my childhood questions about life and death. I now have a sense of knowing that re-enforced my experiences I had through my life prior and shapes my existing beliefs after this experience.

Mattie and I still communicate; it's just in a different way.

★ ★ ★

EPILOGUE

Losing my mom was the hardest thing I have ever experienced. I'm sure anyone who has lost a parent knows that empty feeling in your heart and deep sorrow. The unconditional love that only a parent can give is gone.

I am glad I had the chance to write down the stories of Mattie Fisher, my mom, before she died. As her dementia took hold, I hurried, asking as many questions as possible. In the introduction to this book, I said my original plans were to leave a historical record for Autumn, my daughter and Mattie's granddaughter. But as I dug back into her history, I knew the world had to hear Mattie Fisher's stories.

I hope you found my mom's story and the life lessons I learned from her both powerful and inspirational. I know she naturally inspire the lives of everyone she touched with her grace, her wisdom, her sense of humor and her uncanny "knowing" about the magic that influenced her so many times. I would love to say I immediately took her life lessons to heart, but in good conscience I cannot.

Three years after my mom's death, I married my fiancé on her birthday, May 13th. The wedding took place in our home and a lot of things went wrong that day. Our officiate, my cousin George, was a couple hours late. He arrived without his reading glasses and stumbled through the wedding vows. Then, the cake started wilting and the fruit began turning brown. It was as if the universe was trying to tell me something. I was not listening.

With the marriage, I inherited two adult children and, over the years, five beautiful grandkids. The marriage wasn't perfect, but I put a bandage on it and kept going.

⁓☆⌒⌒⁓☆⌒⌒⁓☆⌒⌒

In the summer of 2001 we added a new edition to our family, Royce the dog. Royce is a high-spirited, precocious, reddish-brown miniature pinscher. In the beginning, I fought against having another mouth to feed and care for under our roof. However, my hesitation was short lived as I fell in love with him very fast. Now, I had another child to look after and I loved every moment of it.

In September 2001 my daughter Autumn and I had the opportunity to go to Madison Square Gardens to see Michael Jackson's 40th Anniversary Concert. We flew from Kansas City to New York City on September 6th. It was all I could do to get my daughter on the airplane that day. She kept telling me she had an odd feeling the plane was going to crash. I chalked up her fears to the plane crash that killed young singer Aaliyah just two weeks earlier. I tried to comfort her by telling her I had prayed and meditated on flying that day. If there was any true danger, the Universe would block us from boarding that plane. She calmed down some and became cautiously optimistic. I gave her a Dramamine and she fell asleep by the time the plane got in the air.

On September 7th, the day of the concert, we spent the morning sightseeing in New York. We walked to the Empire State Building.

I asked Autumn if she wanted to go to the top.

She replied, "No, I'm scared something might happen."

I said okay. Instead we got on a double decker bus for a tour of the city. When we neared the drop-off point for the passengers who wanted to see the Statue of Liberty in the harbor Autumn and I moved to the top of the bus. As the bus pulled off, we saw the World Trade Center twin towers glistening in the sunlight. It was a beautiful sight. So beautiful I had to take a photo of my daughter with the towers as the backdrop.

The concert was magical as only Michael Jackson could create. I wanted to go a show scheduled for Monday September 10th. Luther Vandross was going to be singing that night and I really wanted to see him. That meant I would need a ticket for the show and the ticket counter said they were sold out. If I had been able to purchase a ticket, it meant we would have to change our return flight day to Tuesday September 11th.

We were fortunate Autumn's cousin lives in New York City. She acted as our tour guide on Saturday September 8th. That morning we hit the New York subways headed down for The World Trade Center and shopping at Century 21 across from the twin towers for my daughter's 16th birthday.

When we arrived, I asked Autumn, "Would you like to go to the observatory on top?"

She shook her head violently and said, "No way, mom."

After shopping I asked her again, "Are you sure you wouldn't like to go to the top of the Twin Towers and look out at the city?"

She told me, "Mom, I'm afraid something bad is going to happen."

"Happen; like what?" I asked her.

Autumn's response "I don't know I just think something bad going to happen."

After that we left the area for So Ho.

We left New York City in the early morning hours on Sunday, September 9, 2001 flying back to Kansas City.

As a Federal Employee on September 11th, I was sent home around 11:00 am, devastated at the news of the terrorist attacks. Autumn was on a field trip with her school. I knew she was safe, but I paced the floor as the hours ticked by before I could pick her up. I knew she would be devastated to hear the news, too. I sat waiting in the car outside her high school, thinking about what she said while we were in New York City just two days earlier. Somehow, she knew something was going to happen that involved airplanes and high buildings. When Autumn finally got in the car, her eyes were red from crying. She said," I knew something was wrong."

Autumn inherited the spiritual gifts of precognition from her Granny and me. Also, like me, she only gets glimpses or feelings about something that might happen. But she doesn't get anything specific enough to make predictions. It's frustrating and upsetting when you want to help but can't. We are still moved to tears every September 11 when we consider what could have happened if the days were different or if my concert aspirations to see Luther Vandross came true.

In 2002, I could no longer put bandages on my failing marriage. It seemed like I was reliving my Mom's life, with my Father; failed marriage number two. I could not solve his mental issues and need to remove my daughter from the situation. After spending 13 years with him, I realized I had no idea who he was and what he was capable of doing.

I finally filed for divorce. I spent much of 2002-2003 in and out of court getting restraining orders. Finally, in April 2003 the divorce was granted. The divorce meant leaving my grandkids behind. I was afraid they would think I had abandoned them and I never loved them in the first place. They were too young at the time to truly understand.

I could not keep them in my life without be pulled back in to his madness. Though I'm not in their lives physically, they have always remained a part of me spiritually. I have never stopped praying for them. Katonya, Brian, Michaela, Xander and Maya I love you with all my heart.

Now I'm approaching age 55 and reassessing my life. I have reflected on my hit and miss relationships since my divorce. Specifically, I have thought a great deal about my two failed marriages. Writing this book has led to my own self-discovery process. Could I, like my mom, suffer from Father Hunger?

Even though my father was in my life until his passing, I did not understand him, and it was always an emotionally distant relationship. The men I married were emotionally distant as well. Much of my time was spent chasing their love, time, and attention. They both were family-oriented men which I recognize was my major attraction to them. I craved a big warm family and feared abandonment. They were both very dedicated to their families. Somehow I always envisioned myself nestled up in the loving embrace of family. The problem was, growing up I never saw what a true partnership between a husband and wife looked like. I only knew what abandonment, deceit and sadness looked like. They were men dedicated to their family; I simply was not the family they cared for. I knew it and walked right into it anyway.

In the end I was abandoned, too. I received exactly what I felt inside. As long as I broadcast that abandonment signal out to the universe that is what I received in return. I had to discover how to love and respect myself. I had to learn how to treat myself the way I want others to treat me. *Life lesson learned.*

∽☆✺∽✺∽☆✺∽✺∽☆✺∽

After my divorce, I bought a brand new home on a golf course. I always wanted a newly constructed home, and I finally made my dream come true. I had fun picking out the carpet, the floor stain, and the tiles. I felt peaceful for the first time in a very long time. I threw myself into work.

My daughter had a very busy life as well. She was a competitive dancer and on the dance team at her high school. Autumn was an honor student, typically with multiple honors classes. She graduated from high school and received an academic scholarship to Rockhurst University. No mom could have been prouder when she graduated from college. I felt the presence of my mom next to me in the auditorium that day. After they called Autumn's name I closed my eyes and said, "Mom, I did it." Mom told me in spirit she was proud of me and my tenacity.

While Autumn was in college I asked her father, Tim, if he knew any non-profit organizations I could get involved with. He said, "Yes, the organization I'm involved with needs help." The non-profit is called "Black Family Technology Awareness Association" (BFTAA). Their mission is to bring the Urban Core up to date with the general population in Science Technology Engineering Math (STEM). Volunteering for BFTAA became a family affair as Autumn joined her father and I helping out where we can.

2012 marks twenty years since my mother's death. It has been a journey that has taken all these twenty years to finally begin to understand myself, most of which my mom knew instinctively. In the 1990s, Tony Robbins' "Power Talk" tapes with guests like Dr. Wayne Dyer and Deepak Chopra introduced me to the concept of the mind, body, and spirit connection. I have grown a little each year knowing with certainty that I can control my destiny.

Slowly, I began to understand why mom kept the Holy Bible and the Power of Positive Thinking on her nightstand next to her bed. Mom knew all along. She was so far ahead of her time.

This is a very exciting year. I am releasing this book, but I am also retiring from my career of thirty years. Plus, I will have an empty nest for the first time after twenty-six years.

My family's health struggles with hypertension and its risk factors leading to heart disease and diabetes, so common in the African-American community, guide me to live differently. I now am learning to live an Ayurvedic lifestyle. I hope to introduce this lifestyle to more people soon. I am excited about my new journey as life unfolds before me.

Believe in the Magic

★ ★ ★

www.ingramcontent.com/pod-product-compliance
Lightning Source LLC
LaVergne TN
LVHW091253080426
835510LV00007B/249